D0077112

PUTTING YOUR VALUES TO WORK

PUTTING YOUR VALUES TO WORK

Becoming the Leader Others Want to Follow

Matthew R. Fairholm

 PRAEGER

AN IMPRINT OF ABC-CLIO, LLC
Santa Barbara, California • Denver, Colorado • Oxford, England

Library of Congress Cataloging-in-Publication Data

Fairholm, Matthew R.
   Putting your values to work : becoming the leader others want to follow / Matthew R. Fairholm.
     pages cm
   Includes bibliographical references and index.
   ISBN 978–1–4408–3059–4 (hardback) — ISBN 978–1–4408–3060–0 (e-book)
1. Leadership. 2. Values. I. Title.
HD57.7.F35267   2013
658.4′092—dc23   2013020364

ISBN: 978–1–4408–3059–4
EISBN: 978–1–4408–3060–0

17 16 15 14 13   1 2 3 4 5

This book is also available on the World Wide Web as an eBook.
Visit www.abc-clio.com for details.

Praeger
An Imprint of ABC-CLIO, LLC

ABC-CLIO, LLC
130 Cremona Drive, P.O. Box 1911
Santa Barbara, California 93116-1911

This book is printed on acid-free paper ∞

Manufactured in the United States of America

Contents

Tables and Figures

Tables

Figures

Acknowledgments

I am grateful for the examples, ideas, theories, practices, and principles of others, which have become so integrated into my own reflections on leadership that it is often hard to know which came from me and which came from them. Truly, others have influenced my life for good and helped me be better because of their leadership. Not the least of these individuals includes those of my family, extended and immediate. The family I grew up with had profound and meaningful impacts in my life. Likewise, my family now are indeed the leaders I want to follow as I try to refine my own efforts at leadership. To my wife, Shannon, and my sons, Carl, Benjamin, Nathan, and William, I express my love, my admiration, and my thanks. Indeed, thank you all for your examples and your love.

Chapter 1

Introduction

Years ago, my five-year-old son climbed into my bed *after* the scheduled bedtime. He wanted to snuggle. Wanting to be firm, but also, frankly, wanting to snuggle myself, I decided to make a deal with him. I reminded him that I spend some of my time thinking about leadership. He said he knew. Then came the deal: "If you can answer one question for me, we can snuggle a little bit tonight." He agreed. "Son," I asked, "what is a leader?" He thought for a little while and then, probably thinking about the follow-the-leader game they often played in preschool or maybe the coveted line leader honor given to one of the students before lunch, he looked at me thoughtfully and said, "Dad, a leader is someone who has followers."

I thought then, and think now, just how profound that statement is. It is common sense; it is real life; it just seems so logical. Haven't we all known people who fancied themselves as leaders, but no one chose to follow them? We might call them an entrepreneur at best, but deluded at worst. Leaders have followers. If no one follows, there is no leader and hence no leadership.

But this flies in the face of a long history of leadership thought and research. For decades, we have studied the traits of leaders, the behaviors of leaders, and the processes and situations in which leaders operate. And for decades we have assumed that leaders were those at the head of an organization, group, company, or institution. Whether people willingly followed or not, they were leaders. The foundation of this assumption is that *position* defines leadership.

In reality, though, position is not the foundation of leadership. Power is not even the foundation of leadership. Headship is not necessarily leadership.

Relationship is though. Forming and integrating relationships among programs, missions, goals, values, and, most importantly, people is the stuff of leadership.

Hence, leadership may be better understood not by looking at the privileges and responsibilities of position and headship but rather by considering why someone would choose to follow someone else regardless of the rank, title, position, expertise, or credentials of either the leader or the follower. What is it that makes people choose to follow, to emulate, to support, to serve? And why will people follow some but not others? Answers to these questions are what this book is about. In this chapter, I will briefly discuss the ideas that have inclined us toward a definition of leadership based on position and power. I then argue that that definition is incomplete, if even correct at all. I will explain how a fundamental shift occurred to allow for a conception of leadership that takes a more personal and relational approach to understanding and doing what leadership has really always been.

Problems and Issues of Control

It is not hard to see how we got to the point where leadership seems to be all about power, position, and expertise—the take-charge person who has the answers. One reason is because leaders are supposed to have the answers and solve the problems. The second and third reasons are that leaders are supposed to bring calm to chaos, and they are supposed to control the situation. They are the kinds of people whom everyone looks to in difficult times. They are the ones who are bigger than life, people we can rely on when we can't or won't rely on ourselves. I admit this appeals to me as well. But I don't always follow problem solvers; I follow people I would like to emulate, and if they solve problems, I probably wish I could solve problems like they do or I hope that they would solve problems in ways I agree with. And I can certainly think of people who solve problems who I would not follow. They don't solve them in a way that appeals to my way of doing things or to my beliefs about things. Taking charge, solving problems, and being in a position of power is not enough. Something else has to be there, something that causes me to commit to certain leaders and their way of being and doing.

A professor of leadership at Harvard University, Ron Heifetz, devoted research to the notion of leadership, management, and problem solving. Coming from a medical background and steeped in the techniques and theories of diagnosis and treatment, Heifetz explained the problem-solving role of leaders. One of his insights is about the nature of problems themselves (see Table 1.1). He described Type I problems as those problems whose definitions are clear and whose solution and implementation are clear as well. An example might be that a local government's building permit process is too cumbersome and lengthy. The problem can be analyzed,

TABLE 1.1. Three Types of Problems

	Problem Definition	Solution & Implementation	Kind of Work
Type I	Clear	Clear	Technical/managerial
Type II	Clear	Requires learning	Technical/managerial & adaptive/leadership
Type III	Requires learning	Requires learning	Adaptive/leadership

defined, and resolved using fairly technical, routine, process-control techniques. Is it easy? It may not be, but it is doable and is an example of Type I problems we face frequently in organizations. A key to remember, though, is the kind of work needed to resolve the problem: routine, technical, managerial work.

Type II problems are those whose definitions are clear but whose solutions and implementation are unclear. An example might be an employee whose consistent absenteeism is causing work to be delayed, left undone, or rushed. A manager may be able to define the organizational problem (absenteeism and poor performance). But the solution and how to go about doing what the solution requires may be more involved. Certainly, the employee can be fired. But beyond that solution (which, in essence, is turning the issue into a Type I problem), there are many potential avenues to consider. The manager can talk with the employee or other coworkers to find out what they think the best solution is. The manager can refer the employee to an employee assistance program. The manager can develop work goals and keep checking up on this employee, or offer to pay for time management training, or change the work schedule to accommodate time demands. There are many possible solutions, all requiring different implementation plans. What is clear is that the work of the manager begins to involve more than just technical, routine, controllable processes, though these are involved. When people (and people issues) enter the picture, then adaptive work, relationship work, and creativity enter the picture as well. The kind of work differs between the types of problems.

Type III problems further impact the kind of work involved for the manager. These problems have no clear definition and no clear solution or implementation. For example, the problems of poverty, homelessness, national security, and the like defy easy description and easy answers. I remember working with dedicated people in the Inter-American Development Bank (IDB). One of their missions was to reduce poverty in Latin

America. Much of company time was devoted to understanding and simply defining poverty and its corresponding issues and causes just to figure out the projects and plans needed to help resolve the problem, not to mention, of course, the hard work of then implementing the plans. In fact, these types of problems defy much of the routine, controllable work that managers rely on to get things done. They rely rather on creative, political, analytical, interactive, relational, and adaptive work to come to agreement on both the issues and the potential plans to resolve them. In the IDB example, I was often impressed with how analysis and project management skills were coupled with the cultural and political savvy required in different countries and regions of the world. More than mere technical and routine skills was required, however. Another absolutely essential requirement, as I heard it described, is knowing how to influence others, how to earn trust, how to teach, and how to adapt to cultural norms—the soft skills. Even implementing the plans involves considerable adaptive work because too many variables exist to merely engage in controlled processes to fix the problem.

This taxonomy of problems highlights two kinds of work involved in organizations: management and leadership. Although more will be said on this, it is clear from the start that management work is well suited to dealing with technical and routine problems, while leadership work is better suited to dealing with the uncertain work emerging in organizational life. However, let us remind ourselves that leadership is often confused as being the same as management. Even in dealing with Type II and III problems, rational managers recognize the impossibility of clear definitions and solutions to the actual problem, so they begin the work of defining Type II and III problems as if they were Type I problems and then engage in management, that is, technical work, to resolve them.

For instance, because poverty is too complex to actually deal with holistically, we simply choose to define it, perhaps, as caused by a lack of educational opportunities. Then we begin to develop educational programs and deliver them to those we define as needing them—the high-risk citizens identified through some calculated means test. In so doing, however, we can see that the problem of poverty (a Type III problem) is not actually solved. Rather, the more manageable problem of delivering specific educational programs to specific clientele is resolved, and we hold out hope that such work will have some impact on poverty. Managers do this all the time, and they should, because managers solve problems. This is a rational and perhaps very appropriate way to deal with uncertainty and ambiguity, but alone it will never get us to the solutions to the problems that defy techni-cal, managerial mind-sets. It is, though, one reason why leaders are thought of as problem solvers; leaders are thought to be managers doing managerial work.

The kinds of efforts used to deal with ambiguity and uncertainty are an indicator of whether management or leadership is in play. Consider the typical management activity of planning. Traditionally, planning models have included some notion of scanning the environment, determining important steps to take to fulfill goals and missions, determining measures of success, and encouraging the review of work and achievements.

Whitewater canoeing provides a nice metaphor for the process. Let's say my friend and I enter the river in our canoe, taking in all the beauty of the area, excited about the possibilities. We paddle down the river, letting the current take us along, but not yielding total control to the river current. We have milestones ahead of us, and we make sure we notice and steer clear of the sandbars or logs in the river. We talk of how we can work together better and what we will do when the whitewater rapids draw nearer. We begin to read the river for changes in current, V-shapes in the water (indicating rocks), and other indicators of whitewater ahead. Then we enter the whitewater and put our plans into practice. We get more wet than intended and turned around a little more than we want, but we make it through, exhilarated from the effort, praising ourselves for our skill, and wet from the things we couldn't control. As the water calms itself, we calm down too. We analyze what just happened, wonder why all of our plans didn't quite work as well as intended, and refine plans to control for the whitewater in the future. The whitewater canoeing excursion is a useful metaphor for how we want to operate, how we want to plan, in organiza-tions. This is the work of management.

Peter Vaill, a well-known organizational theorist, however, suggests that the whitewater that organizations engage in, plan for, and respond to is occurring with increased rapidity and frequency. The time to regroup and plan in an environment safe from or removed from whitewater itself is gone. Now are the days (and perhaps they always have been) when white-water is constant, consistent, and turbulent. Within organizations, this means that things move faster, with more interactive components of prob-lems and solutions (opportunities, people, "issues," and so forth), more interdependence among the components, more unanticipated consequen-ces, less time to react to events, more sophisticated but less durable solu-tions, less familiar territory at work, and more time spent "between" than "in" familiar territory. Controlling the organizational whitewater and how we work it requires management and control techniques. Living within a world of whitewater requires a capacity to deal with uncertainty and skill at working with little or no control, something management shuns.

The fact is that this metaphor of permanent whitewater reveals that there is more ambiguity and more uncertainties, perceived and real, in organizations than we often acknowledge. The norm in our organizations, then, is reduced predictability, less direct and indirect control, increased complexity of change, and fewer if any places to hide from change. This environment cries out for the mind-set and activities of leadership as opposed to the skills and techniques of management. Management shuns uncertainty in favor of control; leadership recognizes uncertainty and ambiguity as a reality and is able to work within it, and around it, and through it.

Four Leadership Streams and Organizational Practice

The person in charge, the one at the top of the organization chart, who solves the problem—to whom we look to control chaos, clarify ambiguity, and resolve uncertainty—traditionally uses management skills and techniques. Why we call him or her a leader, actually, is an interesting issue. The foundations of this issue are grounded in both how we have studied leadership and how we have structured organizations.

I have no intention of summarizing the entire history of leadership or organizational thought, but I can mention what I think are some highlights. Let's start around the turn of the last century, when industrial and bureaucratic organizations emerged as a result of the Industrial Revolution, and issues of leadership became a topic of academic study. The Industrial Revolution did a few things relevant to the topics at hand. First, it spurred the development of organizational structures that went beyond the small family business design, resulting in centralized, hierarchical, and control-oriented organizations (the industrial model of organizations). Second, railroad, steel, banking, and other industries emerged with headquarters in one city and field offices in others. Issues of managing from a distance and controlling employees one may never see or meet inevitably made leaders and researchers scratch their heads. Consequently, leadership became a critical concept to study and replicate so that industries and the inevitable organizations that emerged in large metropolitan areas could be efficient, effective, and successful.

The typical industrial organization consists of leaders at the top, managers in the middle, and workers at the bottom. Simplistically, the idea is that

FIGURE 1.1. Traditional Modern Organization and the "Management Line"

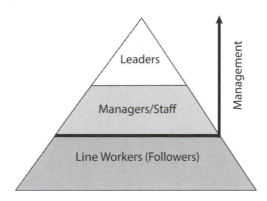

leaders lead, managers ensure things get done, and workers do the work they are told to do by the managers and leaders above them. Managers and leaders began to be the educated, college graduates of the day; laborers came from the noncollege population and those immigrating to the cities from the farms (or from foreign lands). Institutions developed degrees like the MBA (Master of Business Administration) around the turn of the last century (1908 at Harvard), and a decade or two later within government administration the MPA (Master of Public Administration) emerged, to help educate and train management on the basic skills of working with others to get things done well.

Over time, a significant split in organizational life became apparent: the management/labor split (see Figure 1.1). Management (including the ranks of managers and leaders) decided what and how work was to be done. Labor performed the work the way they were told to do it. Management as a function and skill set became based on position, rank, and title. A new class emerged in society different from the population at large: the trained, professional managers. These were the "leaders." Those closer to the top of the organization chart were the better leaders. They were different from others in that they rose to the top, could do what others couldn't do, and embodied traits and characteristics that set them apart. They included the robber barons of the time, the Andrew Carnegies, the Rockefellers, and the J. P. Morgans of the day. They were born to be leaders and took advantage of their supposedly inherent and maybe genetically inherited privileges.

In fact, a leadership research agenda emerged during this time. The question was, What makes some people different from other people in that some are leaders and some are not? Researchers grappled with the question, Are leaders born or made? They answered that if they were not born innately different from others (as some certainly believed), then they were at least born with more of the stuff of leadership than others; they were predisposed to leadership in ways others were not. I recall asking that question to a group of underclassmen: are leaders born or made? One sarcastic student proudly put forth that *all* leaders are born because all people are born. Profound in its sarcasm, the comment was also profound in its summary of much of the results of the research on leadership traits and characteristics. Leaders are different. Birth might not be the differentiating factor, but researchers interviewing and observing those at the top certainly found some characteristics and traits that do tend to predict those who will emerge as leaders and those who will not.

There were studies on height and weight and other physical traits. Taller, more slender men were more likely to be leaders. There were studies on intelligence factors revealing that those with average to above-average intelligence were more likely to be leaders than the super smart or the intelligence challenged. Personality tests, communication skills, emotional intelligence, approaches to achievement, power, and social affiliation were other lines of research that could help us understand what a leader is actually like. If there are fewer people at the top of an organization, and they are the leaders, figuring out what those people are like is a natural course of study. Practically speaking, too, if I want to be a leader, and leaders are at the top, then I want to learn what they are like and develop those traits and characteristics so that I can be at the top too.

While that logic is clear, some thinkers began to wonder whether lists of traits and characteristics are sufficient in describing leadership and proscribing activities. The inability to develop a definitive list of leadership traits that holds true despite person, place, or context worried some. Too many lists emerged and a lack of clarity on leadership continued. Indeed, much knowledge was gained about people at the top, and insights for practice emerged. However, some researchers hoped for more clarity regarding not just what leaders were like but also on what leaders do. They began to focus research efforts on leader behaviors, regardless of personality, intelligence, or height.

This behavioral approach gained popularity and currency, especially after the results of studies conducted at the University of Michigan and The Ohio State University came out. Though independent studies, they looked at similar questions of leader behavior and reported similar results. The interpretations of the data differed, but results suggested two basic behaviors consistent with what leaders (effective leaders) do. Leaders initiate structure; they are task oriented. Leaders also engage in consideration behaviors; they develop relationships. Terms like *autocratic leader*, *democratic leader*, and *laissez-faire leader* entered the vocabulary of leadership studies. Leadership training focused on making high-task leaders better able to engage in behaviors that showed a concern for people and vice versa, turning the people-focused leaders into task-focused ones as well. Truly effective leaders, the theory says, do both very well.

As behavior theory gained advocates and researchers, some began to wonder whether there were times some behaviors were more important than others depending upon the situation. Growing up, I used to read biographies. One of my favorite biographical subjects was Winston Churchill. I wondered why Churchill was considered a great leader during the war years but not during peacetime. He held high office in the United Kingdom, but in the decade before World War II, he struggled to gain either followers or political office. However, during the war, he certainly gained both: followers and high office as prime minister. His influence was vast and his capacity to inspire in those dark days in Britain was the stuff of legend. Though he had one more stint as prime minister in the early 1950s, his influence waned dramatically after the war, and domestic and foreign policy circumstances seemed to work against his political efforts. What did he do differently during the war that he didn't do before the war? Did circumstance make that big a difference in his leadership success? Was one behavior more meaningful, useful, or effective than other behaviors at different times and in different situations?

The new situational leadership theorists asked similar questions more generally. To them, issues of organizational context, external forces, the maturity or competency of subordinates, how decisions were made, which decisions were accepted when, and similar situational issues were more poignant variables than specific behaviors. To them, behaviors were meaningful, in fact, only in the context of the situation or the contingencies at play. The notion of leadership styles emerged during this time. One may have personal preferences, but situations may dictate that a facilitative style is more effective than a directive style, or a coaching style may be more useful than a delegative style. Such findings suggested that leadership depended on various things, such as task competence of leaders and followers, the funding of an organization, organizational life cycles, external factors, internal cohesion, the efficacy of decisions, the need for buy-in, and other interesting issues of context and situation.

Another research stream—and another theory—emerged as people began to wonder whether leadership depended less on traits, behaviors, and situations and more on whether or not someone could actually succeed in getting someone else to follow him or her. Consequently, the research questions changed too. These questions dealt with why some people follow some and not others, rather than with what sets apart people at the top of an organization from those below. This way of looking at leadership is akin to the idea my son mentioned to me as we talked of leadership that one night: leadership is about having followers. So what is it that causes people to choose to follow others? Whatever it is, that is the key to leadership.

This stream of thought is different enough from the other three described above that it deserves some special consideration. A major research assumption of trait theory, behavior theory, or situational theory made by typical researchers is that leaders are found at the top of the organization. We have discussed this before. The leader of a company is the president or the CEO. The leader of a school is the principal or the superintendent. The leader of a city is the mayor and that of the state is the governor. So if we want to study leaders, we should interview, observe, and analyze people at the top of these organizations; or, we should interview, observe, or analyze data from people below *about* the people at the top. Basically, if we study leaders, we will understand leadership.

The leaders-have-followers research agenda, however, rejects this basic assumption. The idea is that if we can understand why some people follow others (leadership), then we can determine who is and who is not a leader. In fact, the very notion of effective leadership is held in question. In the previous research streams, effectiveness was defined more in terms of getting things done. In this stream, an *effective* leader is one who has followers. If one does not have followers, one is not simply ineffective; one is not even a leader. An *effective leader* is therefore redundant. An *ineffective leader* is oxymoronic.

Looking again at the industrial organization model, the first three research streams reinforce the hierarchy and the management line separating managers and leaders from workers. The fourth stream, sometimes called a values-based transformational approach, begins to reject the idea that leadership is equated to position, rank, and title. I once knew an office worker who had no formal position of authority in the organization. He was a regular worker, like everyone else. However, everyone wanted his advice. People gravitated to him for wisdom and insight about new policies, old policies, management transitions, personnel changes, and so forth.

FIGURE 1.2. Leadership Is Independent of Position

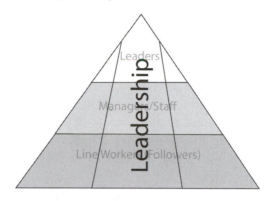

When he spoke, people listened (frequently, even the boss and the boss's boss listened to what he had to say). Indeed, he exerted great influence. Many followed *him* rather than the boss. Sometimes he went in the same direction as the boss, and people followed, which made things easy for the boss. Sometimes he disagreed with the boss, and people followed him instead, which often caused some consternation in the office.

This is an example of the idea that leadership, rather than being dependent upon position, is independent of position (see Figure 1.2). Leadership is relational; management is really the phenomenon based on position. There are some workers who work and some who also do leadership. There are some managers who manage and some who also do leadership. There are leaders who do leadership and there are some leaders who do not do leadership at all but rely only on their position, rank, or title.

What causes someone to follow some people and not others? The values-based transformational theory approach tries to answer that question. The answers lie somewhere in the notions of values and vision and people's voluntary decision to accept a person's explanation or example of specific values, a compelling vision, and certain approaches to the relationship of leader and follower. Indeed, this is the historical stream that informs most of this book.

A Word on Position and Relationships

What we see, then, is that past leadership theory has relied more on position and positional power and authority while ignoring the practical elements of relationship based on something other than position. This point requires clarification. I remember a professor once chided me by saying that managers have a relationship with their employees too, and that it is a little self-serving to a leadership student to suggest that only leaders develop relationships and work in a relationship context. To respond, I would first have to explain the argument made above about the terms *manager* and *management* and concede that many managers do engage in leadership, but not when they are engaging in management. Second, it is the *nature* of the relationship, the purpose of the relationship, even the power source upon which the relationship is built that matters. That a relationship merely exists is certainly not sufficient to diagnose that leadership is happening.

If, however, the relationship, or the desire to make relationships, is not present, there is certainly no leadership in play either. James MacGregor Burns wisely concluded that in the past, leadership was defined in terms of power and the exercise of power; but in reality, leadership is not about power. Rather, it is about relationships: people relating to each other and, I would add, people also relating to purpose, programs, priorities, and the like. Burns said that some people interact with others based solely on power devoid of mutually discerned relationships. This power is exerted based on some position held over others. Burns called these people *raw power wielders*. Often history sees these raw power wielders as leaders. But rather than developing a relationship based on mutual respect of the values of each party, raw power wielders merely exert power over others to get what the power wielder alone wants. Such self-serving, egotistical interactions may sometimes be mistaken for leadership, but it isn't leadership. An authentic leadership relationship is based on some sort of recognition of both the leader *and* the follower that the relationship is mutually beneficial to and intentional by both parties, the goal of which is some satisfaction of mutual values, wants, needs, aspirations, or the like.

Position is shorthand for organizational power. If one has rank, title, and position, one has legitimate power. The result is the foundation for management. Certainly, mutual benefit can accrue from relationships that start out in positional terms. A boss can satisfy the needs of a subordinate for food and shelter by trading a week's worth of work for a certain amount of money. In this sense, the transaction has produced value for both leader and follower and can therefore be called a type of leadership. Burns called it *transactional leadership*. However, this intentional and authentic relationship, based on this kind of power, allows for the satisfaction of only certain limited wants and needs for only a limited time, and has no currency beyond the explicit details of the transaction. The limits are defined by the duration of the transaction. Once the transaction ceases to exist or ceases to have mutual benefit, the relationship is over. The relationship between manager and subordinate is certainly a relationship, but it is not one of mutual growth and development. It is merely based on a transaction that is useful for a time.

Leadership intends more than the satisfaction of needs for a time. Leadership has always been about helping others grow, change, develop, see things in new ways, and satisfy deeply held values that cause us to do differently and be better over time. Burns called this kind of leadership *transforming leadership*, as it transforms both leader and follower to higher levels of capacity and even morality, and is what we really mean when we say *leadership* as opposed to the transactional leadership of management. Therefore leadership is based on a different source of power: personal, persuasive power. Leadership is based on voluntary decisions by leader and follower to choose to influence and be influenced. Such power is not based on position at all, but rather on how one person influences another, especially when there is no environment of coercion or punishment for noncompliance.

A Word on Power

In fact, there are many different sources of power. We have alluded to only two: organizationally legitimate power and personal power. Other sources of power may come from coercive capacities, expertise, the ability to give rewards, associations with other influential people, and "dropping names." In other words, power as a concept is the capacity to do something to cause a change in someone or something based on the expectation that certain results could and will occur because of one's stance, particular circumstance, or capabilities.

The word *power* itself teaches us about the notion of power. Take, for example, the Portuguese noun for power: *poder*. The word *poder* is also the Portuguese verb meaning "to be able to." From the same Latin roots we get the English word *power* and a meaning that is highly relevant to leadership ideas. Power is the ability or capacity to influence others. Hence, power is neither negative nor positive in an ethical sense; it is just the capacity to impact, or to influence, others. Furthermore, power thus defined is more pervasive in society than we often think. More people have power than is often recognized. To say that many people have power, however, we have to understand that power is not defined in only one way.

Power is shorthand for different sources of influence that people can tap into, and some people tap into more sources than others. Additionally, some people tap into different ethical sources than others.

For our purposes, though, understanding that power is nothing more than the capacity to influence allows us to recognize that *how* power is used, and *which* power source is used, is more relevant in the leadership calculus than whether one merely "has power." A question: do we exercise power *over* people, using a source of power based on reward or coercive capacities (management); or do we exercise power *with* other people, using a power source of personal rectitude, honor, or expertise (leadership)?

Power is a helpful concept in understanding leadership, but it is not *the* concept. What seems to matter more is the kind of relationship or interaction that emerges as power is used, and upon what foundation that power is based. Do I use power over others to interact in a one-sided way to get what I want regardless of what others want (power wielder)? Do we use power in some civil, mutually beneficial, yet utilitarian exchange of effort so that the boss (who has position over others) gets what he or she wants and the worker gets what he or she wants while recognizing that the wants of both are rarely the same (management)? Do we use power in such a way that both leader and follower agree that certain values and wants and aspirations are mutually beneficial and more desirable than others and then choose to work together to achieve them in a way that changes both for the better (leadership)? The nature and emergence of real relationships based on mutual respect, shared values, and growth becomes a more appropriate and more fundamental concept or indicator of leadership.

In sum, management is positional and leadership is relational. The development and expressions of authentic, moral, and beneficial relationships are the work and purpose of leadership. It is the relationship that causes leadership to be effective amid ambiguity and uncertainty. It is the relationship that encourages links between people, programs, policies, and priorities. It is the relationship that gives leadership its capacity to create and articulate meaning and purpose in organizations and within people. It is the relationship that makes leadership useful in unifying action. It is the relationship that allows leadership to change people's lives for the better.

The Four Vs Introduced

The Four Vs summarize the technology, or practical application, of the craft of such leadership. They are Values, Vision, Vectors, and Voice (see Figure 1.3). The energizing foundation of leadership relationships is the

FIGURE 1.3. Summary of the Four Vs of Leadership

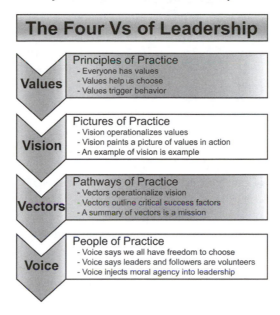

recognition that everyone has values and that values trigger behavior. Values are the first of the Four Vs of Leadership, where each V stands for a critical concept in the technology of leadership. I use the word *technology* on purpose, though it may seem out of place. I take it from the original Greek roots. From the Greek we learn that *techne* is a form of knowledge that is akin to craftsmanship, the ability to engage in a craft. The suffix *-ology* is the study of something. With these two definitions working together, we have a more specific definition of technology that has something to do with the study and efforts of craftsmanship. Technology in this sense is meant to be the systematic treatment of an art or craft; or, similarly, it means the practical application of knowledge.

The Four Vs serve as shorthand for the central elements of leadership. In addition to Values, which is the foundation of the leadership relationship because values form our commitments, ground our choices, and impact our behaviors, the second V is Vision. Vision paints a picture for us of what our values look like in action. Vision helps us see the choices at hand and allows leader and follower to gain a collective view of the cause or purpose that brings them together. Vectors outline critical success factors that help us know the vision is becoming a reality. In a sense, a summary of the vectors comprises the mission for the joint activity. Voice is shorthand for choice. It reminds us that leadership is a voluntary relationship, with leaders and followers having the freedom to choose to be either leaders or followers. Voice further stresses that leadership is an activity of individual agency and free will. The rest of the book will outline each of the Four Vs and link the concepts to the practice of leadership.

Points to Ponder

1. How does focusing on the follower, rather than on individual leaders, help us better understand and define leadership?
2. What kinds of problems do you (or your organization) deal with? Can you identify these problems as Type I, or II, or III? What kind of work do you engage in to deal with or resolve these problems?
3. How are leaders made? Is there sufficient evidence to suggest that some people are just born leaders?
4. Do you think leaders behave differently or more astutely than others in organizational settings? What behaviors do you appreciate in leaders?
5. How might the situation impact leadership? Do traits and behaviors, as well as different situations, matter when we talk about leadership?
6. Does the technology of management differ from the technology of leadership? If so, how?
7. How is it that management relies upon position whereas leadership relies upon relationships? Is there a relationship of management? If so, how might that relationship differ from leadership relationships?
8. Are there some leaders in the organization that don't do leadership? If so, how can that be?
9. How is it that some workers exert more leadership than their bosses?
10. Do leadership and management depend on each other, or are they distinct technologies? In a well-functioning organization, can you have management but no leadership, or leadership but no management? What might be the impact of having only one or the other?
11. How might you define power? Does everyone have power? Are there different kinds of power? If so, what are some examples?
12. How might the Four Vs of Leadership help you understand and do the craft of leadership better?

Quotables

1. "Leaders . . . create a culture supportive of values that lead to mutual growth and enhanced self-determination." —Gil Fairholm, author

2. "If your actions inspire others to dream more, learn more, do more and become more, you are a leader." —John Quincy Adams, sixth president of the United States

3. "To the person who does not know where he wants to go there is no favorable wind." —Seneca

Practical Activities

1. *Problem Types.* Write a list of the problems you or your organization faces. For each problem, determine whether the definition of the problem is clearly defined. Then determine for each problem whether you have a clearly stated and implementable plan to resolve the problem.

2. *Leadership Theories.* List the pros and cons, benefits and pitfalls, of each of the four threads of leadership studies outlined in the chapter: trait theory, behavior theory, situational theory, and values-based transformational theory. Determine which thread you prefer or makes more sense to you. Try to identify someone in your circle of acquaintances who might exemplify each of the theories. Which of these people are you more likely to follow? Why? Does that person's leadership theory match your preferred theory? If not, why not?

Chapter 2

Values: Principles of Practice

The simple idea that "leaders have followers" reminds us that to understand what leadership is, we have to figure out why people follow some and not others. What does it take to get someone to follow you? What occurs to have someone decide to follow someone *else* rather than you? These questions have little (nothing really) to do with rank or title or position in some organization. Certainly, such things yield compliance and obedience—people will do what you say when you have rank—but that is not what we really mean by following someone.

Distinguishing the idea of following from that of obeying is relatively important in an organizational sense. People will do what that manager says without questioning authority as long as the order falls within what Chester Barnard once called the zone of indifference. For Barnard (a businessman, a public administrator, and author of *Functions of the Executive*) the zone of indifference is defined by four criteria. If the criteria are fulfilled, most people will accept the authority of the order and simply do what they are told to do. The first of the four criteria is that the person must be able to understand the order. Second, the person must feel mentally and physically capable of carrying out the order. Third, the person must believe the order is consistent with the organization's purpose. Last, the person must believe the order is consistent with his or her personal interests or goals. Directives that fall within this zone of indifference are obeyed; those falling outside the zone are not. The zone is not fixed over time for individuals, nor do different people necessarily have the same zone. So, indeed, giving orders is not always easy. However, for the most part, management has learned to be pretty good at giving orders that fall within these zones, and people are pretty used to obeying such orders and directives.

Figuring out why people follow as opposed to merely obey, however, includes different criteria. Following has a lot to do with discerning what causes people to behave in certain ways and how people determine certain standards, ideals, or processes for themselves that make sense enough to incorporate into their lives. This brings following into the realm of values. Values trigger behavior. Values act as decision criteria for what we think is worthwhile, important, or even essential for our lives. We decide to follow someone else as we apply our values to the situation. So if leaders have followers (and they do), leaders must work in the environment of followers' values.

Interestingly, we learn more about leadership by understanding what makes followers follow than we do by looking at the leader, his or her traits, behaviors, qualities, and the like. Leadership, therefore, has much to do with people's values and how those values are defined, adopted, and applied. Leaders are inspiring because they are themselves inspired by certain values they feel are appropriate, useful, or right, and then others feel or eventually come to feel the same.

There is no dearth of leadership books. I've perused my share of them, and a few stand out for me. For example, a series of short leadership books written by Max DePree offers nuggets of practical wisdom and profound insight. One such nugget for me was DePree's notion that leadership, in essence, is meddling in people's lives. Such a strong statement is at first a bit shocking especially as it may elicit negative connotations. However, leadership is indeed an act of trying to influence others individually and collectively to do or be or think in certain ways. The leadership task emerges to be one of influencing and integrating behavior and values. If that is not an act of meddling in someone's life, what is?

I have thought much about this notion of the impact leadership has in the lives of others. It begs for a sense of responsibility, integrity, and moral sensibility. Certainly, there are ethical arguments to consider in leadership as well. Such meddling can have profound impacts. That impact, though, is apparent because leadership is an activity that touches the values and underlying principles that guide people's lives. A focus on values must be the starting point for thinking about and doing leadership. Everyone has values, and values trigger behavior. For the sake of being provocative perhaps, but certainly for the sake of clarity and focus, I often say that leadership is, therefore, messing with people's values.

The idea that leadership is messing with people's values is a bit bold and may come across as confrontational or offensive, as my time in leadership development programs has shown me. Often, I begin by introducing the idea that leadership is messing with people's values, and in a spirit of openness I let them know that during the session together I intend to mess with theirs. This statement is a shocking declaration to most of them. Even though I am upfront about my intentions, when I ask if it is okay that I mess with their values, most of them say no. I ask if it is noble of me to be so open about my intentions. They say it is, but they also declare I still won't be able to mess with their values. I reaffirm that I have no intentions of forcing them to believe, but that I do intend to lead them by messing with (or refining, fine-tuning, defining, and so forth) some of their values about organizations, leadership, and getting things done. All in all, they are skeptical, and frankly, I know I take a risk by being so bold.

However, I am still that bold even now because of the experiences I have had in training and in the classroom. People come to realize that messing with people's values is simply another way of saying that people learn and grow and refine themselves through interactions with others and that as long as we are all open about it, they don't feel manipulated or put down; rather, they enjoy the chance to try out new ideas and accept the ones they like. Many participants in such development programs have said they see leadership differently because of the sessions. They see leadership more like I do.

What a responsibility leaders have to be open and, frankly, careful as they work with other people. Ultimately, what results from leadership and messing with people's values is that people change. They see things differently, and they do different things differently because of that change.

This idea that leadership starts with a values foundation reinforces the fundamental notion that leadership is more than technical skill in analyzing, exercising control, and organizing. Rather, leadership deals with people, individual growth and development, and fostering loyalty and commitment to values, even values held by a group. Consequences are not a reliable measure of leadership; relationships are. Those relationships are inherently wrapped around values that are shared or come to be shared by those involved. There is no statement at this point about which values one ought to hold, simply that people group together as they choose to share certain values. I more fully discuss the moral and ethical issues of leadership later.

The Value of Values

The true essence of leadership is not found in procedures. It is in setting and teaching values to followers and inspiring them to agree with, to commit to, and to adopt those values in the work they do and the life they lead.[1] Again, leaders are inspiring because they are themselves inspired by certain values they feel are the most appropriate, useful, or right. Values do a lot for us, and we don't often take the time to realize it.

Some have defined values as social principles, philosophies, goals, and standards of an intrinsic nature. Others say values reflect the essence of who we are and what strongly enriches our lives and therefore they become the core of individuals and of a people. Most of the work on organizational values says that values (perhaps also coupled with attitude) determine— and even dictate—individual and organizational behavior.[2] Values affect the actions a person takes when faced with an opportunity to make a decision and also influence the way a person reacts when confronted with various circumstances and choices. As we learn the significance of choice and decisions in the activities of leadership, we begin to see the pivotal role values play.

Leadership philosophy recognizes the powerful influence a person's individual values set has on the way he or she perceives the world and acts in it. Therefore leadership asks leader, and follower, to deal with each other on a values basis. Though this is not easy, it is essential.

The significance of values is often lost on management and frankly employees. Take, for instance, the result of a nationwide telephone survey of 615 Americans conducted by a Minnesota leadership development firm and reported in *Chief Learning Officer* magazine in 2007.[3] In regard to the question, "Which of the following best describes your attitude toward your own core values and how you earn a living?" the results state that only 44 percent of employees say they know what their core values are and that they are consistent with their employer's core values. Interestingly, 30 percent said they know what their core values are, but they are not always consistent with their employer's. Only 10 percent felt that core values had little or nothing to do with the work they do. That means that 90 percent know that values matter. As the author of the report said, "Management often seems to expect employees to ignore their personal values in favor of the ones posted on the wall . . . It is disconcerting that leaders are not spending more time aligning their employee's values with those of their organization . . . For the individual employee, understanding one's values and being able to work in alignment with them can have a huge impact on performance."[4] Leaders recognize the profound impact of values and are able to identify their own core values and even the values of followers. They are also willing (and able) to shape those values if needed.

Leaders must be comfortable with the preeminent place values hold in the work they do, because leadership depends on those values. Table 2.1

TABLE 2.1. The Value of Values

Important Questions as We Make an Inventory of Our Own Leadership
1. Do I recognize that people have values and that those values trigger behavior?
2. Do I recognize that people bring their values to work?
3. As I try to shape what others in the office are doing, have I given enough emphasis on shaping their values?
4. Do I have a clear sense of my own values?
5. Have I devoted enough time to understanding the organizational and personal values that play out at work?

offers some questions we may ask ourselves to see how we view values in the workplace. Whether leaders explicitly share with followers their core beliefs and values or not, their behavior certainly expresses a personal philosophy and values orientation that they bring with them to the group, to the cause, or to the activity. People see those behaviors and infer the values anyway. We might as well make them explicit.

Morality and Techniques

With this values connotation firmly in our minds, I turn to two important issues. The first deals with the inevitable issues of the morality of leadership, and even some ethical, or morals-in-action, issues. The second deals with how we are supposed to meddle. What is it we do when we engage in leadership that messes with people's values? As you can imagine, a discussion of the first issue guides us in executing the second.

Morality, Motives, and Values

One cannot underestimate the significance of morality as we engage in leadership. Leadership is moral because it deals with values, and our values are an expression or reflection of our morality. Leadership is moral because some of what people do and call *leadership* really isn't leadership, and that may have moral implications as any form of deception or mistaken reality might. A sense of the moral component of leadership helps make the distinction of what is and what is not leadership.

James Macgregor Burns recognized the power of values when he helped define a difference between *transactional leadership* and *transforming leadership* in a book titled *Leadership*, published in 1978.[5] In that discussion, he introduced the concept of how values interconnect with relationships of leadership. Burns suggests we need to disenthrall "ourselves from our overemphasis on power."[6] As with our discussion in chapter 1, he recognized that to equate leadership with power is to lose the distinctive elements of leadership entirely. Relationships between people, not power, is the key. But not just any relationship counts as leadership. Some relationships emerge from doing leadership, and some do not.

In an article titled "The Themes and Theory of Leadership: James MacGregor Burns and the Philosophy of Leadership,"[7] I describe leadership as more than wielding power or manipulating others. It is a moral endeavor. Power, yes, but more importantly "purpose, relationship, motives, and values are essential to leadership because the leader is engaged ultimately in lifting the morals of the follower; in elevating the follower from a lower state to a higher state. In other words, leadership is to help develop others to become moral leaders in the cause of achieving a collective purpose."[8] This is indicative of Burns's overall goal to distill a general theory of moral leadership involving among other elements the values of leaders and followers. Burns says that "leaders with relevant motives and goals of their own respond to the followers' needs and wants and goals in such a way as to meet those motivations and bring changes consonant with those of both leaders and followers, and with the values of both."[9] To make the point even more sharply, he concludes that "to control *things*—tools, mineral resources, money, energy—is an act of power, not leadership, for things have no motives. Power wielders may treat people as things. Leaders may not."[10] He goes on to say that "leadership [is defined] as leaders inducing followers to act for certain goals that represent the values and motivations—the wants and needs, the aspirations and expectations—*of both leaders and followers.*"[11] The genius of leadership, Burns suggests, lies in the manner in which "leaders see and act on their own and their follower's values and motivations."[12]

The article noted above suggests further that "Burns differentiates the practice of using external sources of power and incentives, and internal fountains of commitment and development. In many ways, he differentiates the science of management from the art of leadership and he makes a compelling argument that the two are not the same."[13] Furthermore, it suggests that "leaders address the needs, wants, and values of their followers (as well as their own) and, therefore, serve as an independent force in changing the makeup of the followers' values set."[14] This, he says, is done by gratifying motives and fulfilling values.

Burns describes motives as being "pushed by generalized drives and body-based forces [like survival, hunger, shelter] and pulled by more specific wants, needs, goals, and aspirations."[15] The main source of a person's actions (and decisions to follow) is still some response to internal requirements (what Burns suggests are values) specific to the person.

He says that sometimes people treat values and motives as if they are the same thing—that if they are different at all, it is only in degree, not in type. Burns, however, argues the opposite: that the difference in degree amounts to a real difference in type. The article referenced above notes that "the distinction between motives and values may depend on whether or not the inner drive is merely an expression of need, want, or desire, or whether the inner drive becomes a standard and guide to action toward a desired end-state."[16] Values, those inner drives specific to individuals, are held so deeply that they define personality and attitudes and what an individual is all about. Summarizing the discussion of motives and values, the article states, "In a sense, motives are those drives that are *acted upon* to be satisfied or deprived, while values are those inner drives and commitments that shape or enable us *to act* in certain ways or towards certain end-states."[17] Values, then, serve as goals and standards, modes of behavior, and a representation of instrumental and intrinsic foundations for means and ends. They are significant, therefore, in the activities of leadership, which is getting others to follow.

This discussion of values applies to the social world, the family, the volunteer group, or the work unit, as well as the political or corporate world. In conclusion, the article about Burns's philosophy of leadership defends its argument saying, "Leadership is, at heart, philosophical. It involves a relationship of engagement between the leader and follower based on inner drives, common purpose, and collective needs [wants, and aspirations that define the group]. The key to leadership is the discerning of key values and motives of both the leader and follower and, in accordance to those values, elevating others to a higher sense of performance, fulfillment, autonomy, and purpose."[18]

A ship's captain taught me the way you can manage the behavior of others while remembering to reinforce in others specific values that will guide improved future behavior. He set values, stuck to them, and helped others be just a little bit more consistent with those values when their behavior didn't conform. But it wasn't an easy to lesson to teach. He was in charge of a drug interdiction mission with a typical crew, many of whom were quite new in such service. He established his values and vision and laid out steps to achieve success. The crew responded with a very good record of service, and they were cohesive. However, at one tropical port of call, two of the crew indulged in marijuana—an obviously bad situation for a captain whose mission is drug interdiction. As the crew numbered few and was cohesive, it wasn't long until everyone on board knew. The young captain first managed the situation. He listed the guidelines and regulations and followed established punishments. He did what he had to do. He was fair and just and applied discipline as he needed to. That was all he had to do. He had met the requirements of his position. He managed the situation.

This captain knew there was more to it though. No matter how young these crewmen were, and perhaps because they were young, the captain wanted to help these men learn the proper way to act, the proper values that would cause those behaviors, and why it was important. He didn't have to, but because he was a leader he knew he would. This captain decided to teach and lead these men at the same time he was fulfilling the requirements of his position. He shared how he took the opportunity to reinforce and teach what he thought were essential values to the two crew members and the rest of the crew. He made linkages between the work they do and the purpose of the mission. He connected a vision to the day-to-day work. He taught, reinforced, and lived by example the values important to the success of the crew. He overlaid his management activities with a leadership mind-set that values change behavior more than procedures change behavior. Yes, he did punish the two crewmen, but he also counseled them and taught them. He led them.

His leadership efforts were highlighted less by following procedures and protocol (which he did), but more in terms of the teaching and reinforcing of the values that led the crew to understand the vision of their work better and grasp the true impact of their mission. He helped them choose to be better people by choosing to focus on the values and not merely a set of prescribed actions on board. By doing so, he refined the entire crew's values and thereby changed the crew's behavior for the better. He said the two crewmen came to him separately to thank him and to talk over a few things about life and where they were heading. The mission was even more successful, as he recounted, because the crewmen had changed their views about drugs and their commitment to values, even though they worried about the consequences of their poor choices. That the captain took the opportunity to teach and reinforce overarching values amid managerial punitive actions is a testament to his understanding of what leadership really is.

Values are what help us figure out what counts as true, good, and beautiful. Although these values may emerge from multiple sources—like religion, philosophy, science, secular groups, families, and personal introspection—many of us often do not discuss them and take them for granted for long periods of time. However, there comes a time in people's lives when they need answers to tough questions. These tough times are defined differently by people and vary in degree. National crises, natural disasters, and tragedy close to home certainly count, but so does the feeling that work has lost meaning, that management has it all wrong, that one can't get out of a rut, that one desires to do something useful, that there is hope that something better will come along, or that one should try to *be* better or at least not so bad. Values are both the sources of some of those answers and the results of these internal discussions. People crave clear values statements in difficult times; people cry out for leaders.

John Gardner, in his 1990 book *On Leadership*, says, "Leaders must not only have their own commitments, they must move the rest of us toward commitment. They call us to the sacrifices necessary to achieve our goals. They do not ask more than the community can give, but often ask more than it intended to give or thought it possible to give."[19] I believe the captain knew this too and it guided his interactions with the crew.

Indeed, values serve us in many ways. We use values to choose between things, even when we are not explicitly aware of them. We make choices congruent with our values. True it is that our choices aren't *always* consistent with our values, of course, but when we don't follow our values and convictions we feel bad. We feel remorse, or feel like we did something wrong or inappropriate. We feel inconsistent with what we want ourselves to be, inconsistent with what is right, and inconsistent with our values. When conflict arises within ourselves or among people, it is our values that prompt us how and whether to resolve it. If we believe in "may the best man win," we probably won't take an appeasing stance in the conflict (especially if I think I am the "best man"). On the other hand, if I believe that a good friend is a treasure to be cherished, I might take a more conciliatory stance to the conflict to preserve the relationship. Our values matter in very practical ways.

For example, we really cannot come to any consensus among people unless we base that consensus upon common and shared values. Often, the word *consensus* is used to denote an agreement when the more precise word to be used may be *compromise*. A compromise is an agreement. As its roots illustrate, though, compromise is a mutual agreement to come to terms with someone else; it is dealing with others "with a promise" of contractual integrity. There is no need for the parties in a compromise to accept the other's premises or values. In fact, both parties probably gave up something they really wanted to get to some workable treatment of the issues to move forward in a multilateral action. All that is needed in a compromise is a promise to live with agreed-upon terms; no effort is required to merge values, grow into a mutual understanding, or recognize and sustain the feelings of either party.

Examining the root of the word gives added evidence that consensus is more than merely agreement or compromise. Consensus is dealing with others with a sense of mutual integrity, with oneness emerging from people who authentically reveal their preferences and feelings about the issues at hand. The Latin root *con*, meaning "with," added to the Latin root *sentire*, meaning "to feel," that make up the term *consensus* reveal the true nature of that kind of interaction. When we have consensus, we feel the same way about things. It may not come at once, but by working together, by revealing preferences, by discussing what is valued and why, we can approach a mutuality of sense, of feeling, and of commitment. That is consensus; it takes effort and time and authenticity of the participants. Compromise does not. It has been said that only as our values are in line with the values of others, truly revealed, can we reach consensus. If agreement is reached any other way, the result is at best a friendly compromise.

Values serve as guiding principles of action, as standards of behavior. They even serve as diagnostic tools. When we are faced with dilemmas at work, values help us both recognize the dilemma for what it is and judge among the various alternatives to resolve the dilemma. Values also have the capacity to push us toward more noble goals, rather than letting accident or instinct or impulse serve as our driving forces. Values let us know what we are inspired by and whether something (like a story or a picture) or someone is inspiring. They help us persevere through difficulty and strive toward something greater.

Attempting to define values is not necessarily easy though. There is a commonsense notion of what values are and that they define us. I like the definition that values tell us or show us what we believe is true, good, and beautiful in the world. Another way to think of values is that they are broad, general beliefs about the way people should behave or some end state that they should attain. Values can be thought of as standards that can be used to establish choices to be made, determine equity, and balance policies and practices. Psychologist Milton Rokeach suggests that values are "an enduring belief that a specific mode of conduct or end state of existence is personally or socially preferable"[20] to an opposing mode of conduct or end state.

Values obviously have an immense impact on people's lives. To risk "messing with" them is a formidable and intimate activity. Leaders have to be careful. Followers have to be careful too. Perhaps the major concerns about engaging with people at a values level may revolve around two ideas: the potential for manipulation and the potential for having wrong or evil values that others shouldn't follow but do anyway.

Manipulation and What Is Wrong

People don't want to be manipulated into believing or doing something contrary to what their true values or goals are. To mess with people's values by manipulating their circumstances, responses, or points of views is not leadership. It is simply manipulation, an act of wielding power over someone. Leadership does not and cannot allow such manipulation to take place. The difference is real choice. In manipulation, real choice by the individual is not present. Alternatives may be ignored or left undiscussed and hidden from view, consequences may be distorted or ignored, and opposing values may be suppressed. Such circumstances and tactics disallow followers to really know the values choices to be made. They have no real choice to choose to follow because the antecedents of real choice are suppressed.

Secrecy in any relationship seems to identify it as manipulation. Writers on manipulation help us unpack manipulation by making distinctions between overt aggression and covert aggression. There are manipulative people who are openly determined to have others choose their way of things. They use a number of tactics designed to make it "inevitable" that people choose to follow them. Overtly aggressive people use coercion or reason, hard or soft tactics, to get others to follow them. These are relatively easy to spot. Hence, the choice to follow or not is clearer. However, if you choose not to follow, the manipulator may paint that choice not to follow in very dire ways. This is the classic technique of the popular kid in high school who suggests that not being in his or her crowd would be devastating to both social status and personal self-worth.

It is the covertly aggressive person who uses underhanded, subtle, and downright deceptive means to impact someone's decision who is commonly labeled a manipulator. Manipulation is an act of duality: claiming one thing but being or doing another. Manipulators' desire for others to follow them or for people to give them what they want is no less than the overt power wielder's desire, but their tactics are sneakier and hence harder to recognize. They show few if any outward signs of aggression or coercion but are still able to intimidate others into following them or giving them what they want. They may feign interest in the other, but their real interests are only self-centered. The relationship, if it can be called a relationship, is one-sided; the concerns and values and aspirations and hopes of only one side of the relationship are considered—those of the other side not at all. There is no mutuality. Such Janus-like, two-faced duality is a mainstay of manipulation.

Leadership doesn't do that. Leadership is open and allows for alternatives to be discussed and to be chosen if the follower desires. Leadership allows for people to choose not to follow. Manipulation intends for people to make only one choice. Manipulation intends others to follow no matter what, but not because of honest choice and consideration. If we don't allow for choice, we are messing with other people's values in an immoral way. Such cannot be considered leadership.

The other concern with the morality of leadership is that the values a leader presents for others to follow may simply be very bad, evil values. Helping others choose to be bad is considered immoral, the argument goes, and it's an easy argument to make. This is trickier than manipulation. If leadership is present, but the values undergirding the leadership effort are bad, then there is a great risk of leading people into improper, unethical, immoral, bad, evil choices or behaviors or beliefs. Unfortunately, this is a real risk. History is replete with examples of people who hold what I would consider immoral or evil values sets leading others into immoral paths. Perhaps your view of history's actors may not yield the same list of evil-doers, if any at all, but the point is simply that leadership is a moral endeavor because there is a chance that leaders may lead in immoral directions. Because a follower has the chance to decide for him or herself what is moral or immoral, good or evil, as he or she chooses to follow, then leadership is deeply concerned with morality.

The moral dilemmas of choosing to follow someone are not a concern for those who suggest there is no way to gauge the morality of any one set of values over another set of values. But for those like me who believe there are some values that are better than other values, this is a great concern. To be clearer, there is right and wrong and there is better and worse. For example, love (a value construct) is better than hate (a value construct), and leading others to love is better than leading them to hate. And, in like manner, many other values can be judged better than other values. For example, there can be judgments made among values like freedom and oppression, domination and subordination, or self-reliance and dependence. Leadership requires a moral stance. But it also requires a commitment to a person's freedom to choose if the relationship is to be one of leadership. The unfortunate moral truth of the matter is that some people will choose to lead grounded in the baser values, and other people will choose to follow those baser values. It is a morally hazardous and risky venture to engage in leadership for sure.

It can be said that if leadership is not grounded in the good and the true and the beautiful, it may not be leadership at all. Certainly, though, as leadership grounds itself in values, the morality of leadership is clear and evident. To summarize, *leadership is moral in that values are central to it.* It is moral because the doing of leadership has moral results. It is moral because, in a real sense, the purpose of leadership is to help us be more moral. I claim here that if the doing of and the result of leadership is not noble and does not lead to more evident and higher-order morality in leader and follower, it may not be leadership at all.

Values Displacement: The Techniques

How do we best use this understanding to refine our techniques and approaches to leadership? This is the second of the two issues to discuss. Milton Rokeach, who spent his academic career studying values, concludes the following about values and how they play out in our lives:

1. The total number of values that any person holds is relatively small.
2. All individuals throughout the world possess the same values to different degrees.
3. Values are organized into value systems.
4. The antecedents of human values can be traced to culture, community, society, and personality.
5. The consequences of human values can be manifested in almost every aspect of individuals' lives.[21]

In other words, values really aren't that mysterious. The idea that we may all have similar values is sometimes hard to accept, especially as we see the diversity of the world. A researcher named Rushworth Kidder, however, lends evidence to the claim.[22] He studied multiple cultures around the world, interviewing people and identifying certain values that those cultures held as common and important. The results included about six universal values with a few honorable mentions. They are as follows: love, unity, truthfulness, tolerance, fairness, responsibility, freedom, and respect for life. The honorable mentions include courage, wisdom, hospitality, peace, and obedience.[23]

Values Sets

Perhaps in a general sense, we all have fairly similar values. We just organize them in values sets that differ according to our relative rankings of those values. A values set can be thought of as a complex web of supporting and, at times, conflicting set of values possessed by a person or group of people. For instance, there may be five values at work: A, B, C, D, and E. For me, A is most important, then D, then C, but B and E just aren't very important to me. My values set then could be ranked as A, D, C, B/E. Another person (Person 2) may hold the same values but have a different values set ranking, say D, E, B, A, C. Perhaps leadership, then, on my part, is to help Person 2 learn and agree that A really is more important than previously thought and to help Person 2's values set become A, D, E, B, C. Even more profound influence and leadership would be helping Person 2 believe C is more important than E or B. Then Person 2's values set would become A, D, C, E, B, which looks a lot more like my values set. Figure 2.1 illustrates a way of viewing the process of values displacement in leadership.

As this occurs, the person follows my lead, adopts my values set, and by consequence alters attitudes and behaviors to be congruent with the leader's views, purposes, and ways of doing things. That may explain what it means to meddle in someone's life and why leadership is an act of teaching that changes people (for good, in both quality and duration). A reminder from the previous section tells us that we should hope A, B, C, D, and E are good, not bad, values.

Again, according to Rokeach, values have a transcendental quality that guides an actor's actions, attitudes, and judgments beyond immediate goals to more ultimate ends.[24] Although values are, in some sense, natural and ideal, they are not necessarily mutually supportive. For example, consider the potential contradictions of being thrifty and charitable. Both are viable values with attendant worthy behaviors. But they may tend toward cross-purposes, at least in some points of view. For instance, the thrifty person may interpret thriftiness to mean that he won't give money or resources to charity—his ends are to retain his money and his means are to refrain from giving it out willy-nilly. Although he has a desire to be charitable and defines charity to be generous with money, the person may find himself in conflict because his values may be interpreted to be in conflict.

FIGURE 2.1. Leading Changes in Values Sets

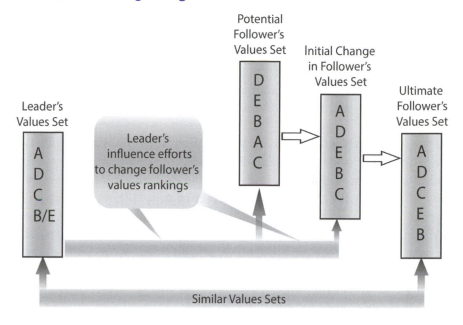

As these value conflicts are resolved, either consciously or subconsciously, a hierarchical arrangement evolves into a value system. A *value system* is simply a rank ordering of values that serves to resolve inter- and intrapersonal conflicts and directs the selection of one alternative way of being from another. Again, such conflicts are very often worked out within the personal introspections and decisions, or the internal conversations, people have with themselves. But these conflicts also play out among people in groups too. So individuals and groups can and do work out values sets.

It is useful to understand that, with respect to leadership, value systems are organized around two main objects. Some values—called *terminal*—refer to desirable end states. Other values—called *instrumental*—refer to modes of conduct. We have already touched a bit on how leadership and values may impact both the end results of behavior and the actual behaviors themselves that will yield the end results. Instrumental values are those that become the tools we use to achieve desired ends. For example, I might believe that a life in pursuit of wisdom is a valuable end state, or terminal value. Intellectual honesty, study, and a reliance on faith and corresponding works might be the instrumental values that help me get there.

The discernment of values sets gives individuals the opportunity to think about what they value the most and why. It allows them to gain a deeper self-knowledge and self-awareness that can contribute to positive achievement, and help them to identify and develop their strengths and gifts. It also gives them the opportunity to see that there are many other values that others can hold. This understanding can help people be in harmony with others and especially help in creating meaningful relationships—the stuff of leadership.

The idea of values sets helps us get a grip on how values shape who we are individually while at the same time giving us the foundation to shape collective activity and identity. We are unique individuals with unique values sets. But we also choose to join together in collective activity based on our individual values sets, which ultimately creates a collective set of values. Some may call that a *culture*. Joining together does not cause me to lose my identity. In fact, it is my unique identity, defined by my values and personal goals, that causes me to join with some and not with others. Indeed, values are powerful forces that impact our attitudes and behavior. Rather than emerging from culture and societal norms, my argument is that values help create culture and societal norms as well.

Certainly, there is some measure of push and pull between individual values and collective norms, but individuals make up groups and societies, and individual values play a key role in a leader's efforts to develop a group culture. If I want to lead others and bring them together in a cause, I start with the individual and his or her values and let the culture merge and reinforce what the individual values or comes to value over time.

Helping others shape both their instrumental and terminal values are key elements of the work of leadership. The question may be, of course, how do you do that? How do you shape other people's values? There are three things to discuss that may help in this effort. The first is to help others come to a common agreement of what the word representing the value actually means. The second is to understand what it takes for something to be a personal value in the first place. The third is to know what you might be able to do if you happen to hold a position of authority in a hierarchy of people organized together.

The Teaching of Values

Words seem simple, but we all know individual interpretation can make words very complex. Take, for example, the value we call *justice*. Seems simple. Believing in justice is a worthy value for many. However, the value *justice*—as in, "I think justice is important"—can mean one thing to one person and another thing to another person. Justice to one may lead him to act in ways that allow people to reap the rewards of their own efforts, because that is just. Justice to someone else may lead her to try to equalize aspects of life, because it would be just that all have the same. To another, justice may lead him to understand that different treatment for different people (because the circumstances and needs are different) is just.

If we begin to add adjectives to help us define justice, then we often get even more complex. For example, if I add the term *social* to *justice*, making *social justice*, then two people who believe in justice may now diverge in their agreement: one may not believe in *social* justice, and the other may hold to it vehemently, perhaps even more passionately than with respect to mere justice alone. For these two people, the adjective may have more power than the noun in the long-term, practical sense. The point is that it is the refining of the value by use of the adjective that really gives significance to the value itself.

When I as a leader espouse a value, I have to be careful to make sure its definition is understood by either my words or my deeds, or both. For example, if a potential leader says we believe in justice, one person may not follow, because opposition to social justice colors any mention of the term *justice* (even if social justice wasn't even mentioned). On the other hand, advocates of social justice may or may not want to follow a leader touting justice until they hear the leader define *justice*, or until they hear an addition of some adjective they could agree with. Leading people to alter their values sets is an act of teaching the nuances of, the adjectives that are put on the terms related to, and the translations and applications deemed relevant or appropriate regarding the values that make up people's values sets.

Another crucial element of leadership is developing the ability to grasp the core beliefs and values of others—the followers. This helps in determining which values are being held in common and what values should be talked about and defined for potential followers. Leaders must always keep constant attention by listening to and watching what the followers both say and do. Leaders do this the same way followers learn the values sets of their leaders: they listen and watch. Through listening and watching, leaders are able to evaluate how comfortable their followers are with the values set of the organization and, in turn, help their followers become better invested in the organizational values.

Listening is not easy. I am reminded of the leader of a mediation team, a professional listener, who complained about how one of her team never listened to her. She thought this was very ironic as mediators are trained to listen. She struggled herself, though, to put her well-honed listening skills into practice with her own team member. She told me that she "consistently said one of the best things you can do as a mediator is 'shut up and listen,'" but even she struggled to listen, to hear, to watch, and to discern the issues of her own team member. No, it isn't always easy to listen, even for trained mediators.

Something that helps, though, is something my father taught me: naïve listening—that is, listening as if you have never heard what is being said before. It requires listening with such interest and focus to the talker that you can't help but show the talker how much you respect her as a person and what she has to say.

I admit, as a teacher myself, I struggle with putting this into practice. It is not uncommon for a teacher to hear the same question from different students time and time again. I know teachers who practice their pat answers whenever a question is even close to one they have heard before. But when I try hard to listen naïvely, as if I have never heard the question before, I realize that actually I never have heard the question before from *that* person, in *that* context, at *that* time. It is a new experience because it is a new person and circumstance. Such listening and watching and conversing are very powerful tools in discerning the values of other people. When I give a person that much respect to listen to what he or she has to say so intently, I can't help but have a meaningful conversation and a jumping-off point to some real mutual understanding and influencing. It is a great way to develop a solid foundation to learn from and especially to teach others.

It is common to suggest that leading is teaching. So what do leaders teach? They teach values, and consequently they teach behaviors, definitions, standards, noble goals, choices, alternatives, and so on that flow from those values. The successful leader teaches the individual the accepted values and lets the followers choose and act for themselves, confident that their actions will not damage the organization because the values are consistent with group objectives. Leadership is really about relationships and teaching; and, because values are the foundation, leadership is about one's character and awareness of self as well.

To Be a Value for Me

An important aspect of teaching then is to be clear on *your* values so you *can* teach them. The same way you make values your own is the way others make values their own. We teach people values when we help them

TABLE 2.2. For Something to Be a Value

- It must be freely chosen from alternatives.
- The effects of the various alternatives must be considered.
- It must be acted upon by the person.
- It must be acted upon enough to understand it well.
- It must help the person achieve his or her potential.
- It must be publicly affirmed.

through this process. The process is outlined below and summarized in Table 2.2.

For something to be a value, it must be freely chosen from alternatives. Voluntary selection is best; in fact, it is the only way leadership is taking place. As a leader, we can and should present the values we want in ways that others will choose them—not through some manipulation or communication sleight of hand, but through honest presentation of alternative ways of being and doing.

The presentation of possible values includes describing the effects, as far as they can be determined, of the various alternatives so that they can be seriously considered. Then there must be an opportunity to act upon the presented values to experience some of the effects or learn new ones. This action is called choosing some values over other values. Leaders need to provide, or even create, opportunities for others to try out the values. Providing a chance to practice what a value is like and how it feels is a key leadership activity.

Acting only once on a possible value, however, is not sufficient. Eventually a person needs to act repeatedly on the value to get a good sense of its impact. Leadership requires that leaders not only are able to convey the values of the organization but also must be able to convey why those values are important to the organization to their followers. It is not enough for individuals to simply verbalize their values, but rather they have to live them out through their daily work. Individuals need to see, feel, or experience that the value and its effects will help them achieve their potential, hopes, aspirations, plans, and so forth. This experience can be personal or vicarious. The value eventually needs to be held in high esteem by the follower, recognizing that the value is helpful and beneficial.

A leader reinforces these experiments on the value. But for the value really to be embedded in someone's way of life, it eventually has to be publicly affirmed. People need to let others know the values they have chosen make sense and are true, good, and beautiful. When that happens, the value is their own.

I recall the story of a new positional leader in a nonprofit, community-based, service-focused organization who inherited a well-functioning group from someone he and most others considered to be a leader. What to do? Everything was going well, and this manager feared he would not live up to the previous leader. After a while, this new leader decided to focus on two basic values he felt would both keep the successes going and enhance both the people and the processes at hand. One of those values was happiness. He talked about happiness, he defined happiness, and he put up posters with the word *happiness* on them, images of happy people displayed, and so forth. He suggested happiness was both a terminal and an instrumental value. And he tried to live up to the value of happiness and help others do the same.

The results were not instantaneous. It was only when he heard others talking about happiness that he knew the value had sunk in. At a meeting (one he attended as an observer, not a participant), the people referred to one of the times the leader (him) had defined happiness and how it applied to the organization. He knew then that people were talking about it. Then he heard through the grapevine that other people had been defending happiness as central to the work being done. In meetings around the organization, the happiness theme was echoed and defended. People were describing to others how this focus had changed the way they viewed their work and gave them a new aspiration to reach. He knew then that at least some people had adopted the value for themselves, as they were standing up for it on their own. He noticed that people smiled more and that they were sharing the success of a happy attitude in their own lives. He also noticed that some people didn't smile much but wanted to, and that others wanted to help. Over time, happiness was not a new idea. It was what the organization was about, and people tried to live it, define it, defend it, and help others live it too. That value had moved from being the leader's focus to a reaffirmed value of the organization and its members.

This kind of thing happens more often than we think. It happened in a small division of the Chinese People's Bank. A few years ago I was made aware of the effort of one Chinese bureaucrat to fix the documented deficiencies in the office by dismissing the traditional management practices of command and control and instituting a values-based approach to getting work done. The newly appointed senior manager interviewed the division's supervisor about his approach to work. The supervisor said that his goals were to improve productivity and efficiency in order to ensure that the routine report his office is responsible for could be delivered to the finance group on time. For that purpose, he really emphasized task accomplishment. He personally observed, measured, and experimented with the workload of each process and procedure to formulate a quota for each subordinate. He came to the office every morning with work assignments for his subordinates, and he created specific criteria to both reward and punish them. In this way, he felt he was teaching them the best work methods while also rewarding them for good work. After some discussion about the supervisor's work and the lack of success as perceived by his superiors, the senior manager recognizing the managerial activities the supervisor engaged in said, "Well, that hasn't worked so well, has it?"

The failure was even more apparent after the senior manager heard from the staff. These were the kinds of comments given to him about the office's work and the supervisor: "The problem is that I'm never quite sure where the work is going. I really hope to have more communication with my group members." "I think he treats me like somebody who doesn't know anything, as if I had no training whatsoever." "Some people treat me as trash, they are trying to fire me."

The senior manager taught the division supervisor about the power of values and suggested the values that the supervisor had been implicitly promoting were ones that caused dissension and frustration and reduced productivity among his subordinates. The senior manager suggested the following:

- Establish *altruistic values* for the group membership as opposed to work product, efficiency standards.
- Shift group goals from mere emphasis on productivity improvement and efficiency to concern for individual growth as well as group productivity.
- Abandon quotas and stop making detailed assignments for group members. Rather, teach them the reasons for the work and the appropriate deadlines.
- Give members autonomy and foster their self-development, creativity, and sense of belonging to a cause.
- Look after the group members' spirits.

The values and principles settled on by the two were *shared goal setting*, *empowerment*, *communication*, and *caring*. Interestingly, the senior manager also counseled the supervisor to encourage group members to "share themselves" by discussing their ways of thinking, their values, their hopes, and their aspirations. Over time they developed trust, and smoother work processes emerged. Division members believed that a kind of informal, comfortable, and nonthreatening group atmosphere or culture was created.

They began to express an appreciation for these new values and even defended them within the more traditional structures of their organization.

One staff member said, "People in this group care; the supervisor has come to respect others." Another said that real communication was finally taking place in the group and that the need to belong was being satisfied. Another mentioned that now he knew the goal of the work, rather than just being required to obey the directions and orders of his supervisor. Still another expressed love for the group, calling it like a family wherein the last two months (of the change effort) the group members gave him a great deal of "warmth" and "personal attention." In his words, they seemed to see his good qualities that no one else seemed to sense, and the team was tolerant, understanding, and accepting of his feelings, even when he expressed anger, impatience, or dejection. One worker said the group sympathized with his troubles, yet they also involved him in discussing work problems seeking to know what he could do to help. This employee felt obligated to give his best to the team, as a way to express thanks for their help and concern.

Although the transition to this values-based approach was not instantaneous, just two months after the new approach the bank issued a letter praising their improved performance and recognizing the new kind of leadership as a model to adopt in the larger organization. Last I knew, the adoption of this leadership approach had not happened in the larger bank setting. In fact, my colleague said even a year later it was still hard for the group to maintain such a focus amid the managerial pressures of the other divisions with which they interacted. But that group had learned to appreciate values different than mere efficiency and productivity; furthermore, they not only adopted it themselves, but they also defended it to others. They learned alternative values and approaches to work, tried them out, and experienced the new values; and over time, they saw the benefits that came from them, and they defended the values and new approach to work even in the face of counterpressure. Such is the power of leadership to impact performance and behavior by focusing on and adopting certain values over others.

A leader builds environments that encourage discussion among people to help them defend and support the emerging values. They create situations where the value can be seen as a guiding principle to proper and successful action. Leaders encourage followers to act on the values in isolated situations. They need to act on the value when no one else is looking, when they really could do anything else. Of course, a leader cannot really know if

TABLE 2.3 Nonpositional Ways to Change Values

- Choosing the value: Explain and couch the values you want in ways that others will choose them; voluntary selection is the key.
- Acting upon the value once or twice: Provide opportunities (via projects, social situations, work flow changes, training, etc.) for others to try them out.
- Acting according to a routine pattern: Incorporate the value(s) into all appropriate activities and remind people of the values that ground the activities.
- Esteeming: Help others see that the new value(s) is helpful and benefits them (via storytelling, coaching interviews, outside reviews, personal growth, etc.).
- Publicly affirming: Build discussion among people to help them defend and support the emerging value(s).
- Acting in isolated situations: Create situations where the value(s) can be seen as a guiding principle to proper, successful action.

that private activity is occurring; otherwise, it wouldn't be private. But there needs to be a sense that the value is being practiced even when the leader is not around. The leader might have a creative way to encourage scenarios wherein such private value application can take place.

I remember one minster who wanted to encourage the youth in his congregation to pray more in private, on their own, and at the side of their bed, so to speak. He talked about the "callused knees club," a reference to calluses that form on a person's knees when he or she is kneeling down to pray on a consistent basis. This creative approach was a simple, and maybe even silly, way to encourage the youth to pray more often on their own. But it also provided a unique way of checking to see if it was happening. Table 2.3 summarizes the six ideal phases of changing values.

Being in Charge . . . and Leading

Coupled with this need for private practice is a leader's opportunity to routinize the incorporation of the values within the organization. Meetings, forms, group activities, the way we send and receive information, how decisions are made, and so forth should reinforce the values and allow followers to routinely practice such values. In fact, evidence that values are being practiced privately is the degree to which it is easy for followers to practice the values publicly in the more formal, routinized, and public forums the organization presents.

To spark the values of others, a leader must know what makes individuals excited and use that knowledge to create a link between personal values and the corporate values. One leadership researcher suggests that if

TABLE 2.4 Positional Activities to Change Values

- Publish a new code of values: create a new standard of belief.
- Hire a new boss: abruptly end previously held values orientations.
- Make status quo boring: slowly withdraw impact of previous effort and values.
- Train and cross-train: specify explicit contexts where new values are applicable; rationalize; cause values to be seen in new situations or spheres of influence.
- Control the environment: limit confrontation of the new values with other opposing values.
- Persuade: explain an implicit value and its positive potential.
- Adopt new policies and procedures: create a greater systematic application of a value in many circumstances.
- Force focus: intensify a value from one among many to the center of our life/work.

employees within a company do not share beliefs and values similar to those of the organization, they may unintentionally work against the values established by the institution.[25] It is useful and beneficial to have a difference in opinion and skills among the workforce, but the success of an organization depends not merely on the diversity of skills but also on the unity of purpose.

There are a few activities or techniques to keep in mind in creating this more formal, routinized, and public effort to teach and reinforce values (see Table 2.4). These efforts often require a position of authority to make happen. They show that we can teach values even within a formal organization that may have had different values. For example, a boss may simply publish a new code of values. In this way, the boss is beginning to outline a new standard of belief and action, which is an initial step in getting followers to know what new options are out there for them to try out. The organization's higher-ups could simply hire a new boss with a whole new outlook on work and people and things. In this way, the hierarchy is abruptly ending the previously held value orientations and announcing in a forceful way that the old way of doing things isn't going to be the new way. Of course, the new boss has to exemplify the desired new values. Another way would be for a boss to adopt new policies and procedures—those that reinforce the activities and behaviors intended by the new values set. This adoption would allow for a systematic application of a value in many circumstances throughout the organization.

Bosses can also exert leadership in terms of teaching and reinforcing values by controlling the environment. Because of the formal authority, bosses have a chance to control, in some sense, what is being focused on and what is not (at least formally). In this way, there can be limits placed on any confrontations that emerge between the new values and the old or opposing values. Discussions can be started and discussions can be stopped, thus intensifying one value or a set of new values beyond others. These discussions highlight the new values as central to our work and, perhaps, even of our lives. Of course, because of the span of influence that hierarchical positions offer, bosses can also be more persuasive about the implicit worth of some values as opposed to other values. Part of that may include an effort to make the current status quo boring and unfulfilling so that the new values are more energizing and exciting. This slow withdrawal of previous efforts attached to previous values goes a long way in inculcating new values and new corresponding efforts.

Linked to many of these efforts may be the introduction of a training program that is based on and reinforces new values. Such training would present specific and explicit contexts in which the new values are applicable and outline the potential outcomes of the new values. Training across areas and among a variety of organizational interests would also help people see the values in new situations and spheres of influence, thus giving even more credence to the worth of the new values sets.

One time I had the opportunity to restructure a formal process that was central to the work the organization did. My challenge was to help others rethink the way they did their work and to begin to value cooperation and information sharing across previously related, but isolated, functions. The organization was divided into three general areas of service. Each area covered similar topics of interest but dealt with unique and different clientele. Information could be shared for the benefit of all involved, but it was necessary that such information actually be shared. Often, it wasn't. Some service areas knew things other service areas didn't. Not always, but often enough, the lack of information sharing caused problems for the entire organization. A new boss entered the picture. He wanted to solve the lack of information sharing to gain the synergies that better cooperation could provide.

That became my project: restructure and redesign the work flow and make it last. I was asked to change the work and the work culture. I realized that this was going to be an intimate activity, even though it seemed like a simple work redesign. Whatever I did would require people to change their current ways of operating, to work with people they really never had to work with before, and to have their performance appraised in conjunction with other people's efforts, not just their own. If that isn't personal, what is?

Though I really didn't know it at the time, I was engaging in a values-transformation project. I had to help people see benefits in new ways of operating and to believe that cooperation and sharing and other great values were better than the ones that formed the foundation of the current way of doing business. Looking back, I realized that this effort was a values-change effort undertaken by someone in authority (the boss) through me, someone who had no formal authority other than that delegated to me from above. Over time, we did change from a functionally designed organization to what could be called in today's vocabulary a *matrixed organization*. We were organized by issue area with groups composed of representatives from all three service areas who had to meet together weekly to coordinate efforts and to compile an issues and performance report to be given to the boss.

The change was not easy, but the values were taught, tried out, privately examined, publicly affirmed, and behaviorally adopted. A number of techniques were used, but I remember one in particular, as it seemed to be the most obvious environmental change intended to reinforce the values change. It was completely at the boss's discretion and instituted under his authority: we changed the agenda and process of weekly staff meetings— not rocket science, but a tremendous way to reinforce a new values set. Instead of staff meetings involving individuals sharing accomplishments and highlighting future areas of concern, the boss had each issue group (I believe there were eight we devised) choose a representative to discuss the group's accomplishments and future issues of concern. That one change caused individuals to think in terms of the group, rather than of only themselves. It caused reports and issues to take into account all service areas and not just one, and it required that the group members talk to each other and coordinate information beforehand so the staff meeting would be efficient and useful to the organization. It was a relatively simple change that altered the work and the work culture. It accomplished that change, I realized later, because what was valued at work had changed. The people had learned to accept the new values context. Perhaps this story is more about generic change efforts in organizations, but it helped me realize that all organizational change is essentially people change; and people change is about values change.

Whether personal and intimate or organizational and formal, leadership is at least partly about teaching and presenting values to people in a way that they will ultimately see the benefit of those values and be sure enough of them to let others know about the values. It is about getting others to choose one way over another and realize that the "other way" is based on values that are worthy and useful and represent something better.

Principles Are Important

Values have always been operationalized into what we call *principles*. Indeed, if leadership is a values-based phenomenon, it is also a principle-based endeavor. In fact, the idea of principle is even more specific to the leadership activity, especially as we understand leadership to be a moral endeavor as described above. A principle is a moral and intellectual foundation upon which to act, knowing that the action that is taken will have accompanying results, rewards, or outcomes related to the moral or intellectual truths forming the foundation. It is a statement of truth with a promise of particular results.

The word *principle* is derived from roots that indicate the idea of beginnings, first parts, origins, and sources. It relates to the idea of fundamental truths that are the beginnings of action. The truths or values espoused are not merely good to know or believe, but are good reasons to act. The greater the truth found in the principles, the greater the action and accompanying results. Indeed the principle impels one to act in certain ways to be congruent with the truth and to reap the rewards that such truth may imply or ensure. Furthermore, principles cause us *not* to do some things because the truth found within them warns us that contrary action will not result in the intended results.

For example, one principle—that we reap what we sow—encourages a farmer to plant corn seeds if the desired outcome is corn; a farmer does not plant soy bean seeds if the desired goal is corn. Of course, if the farmer does plant soy bean seeds, the principle suggests the farmer should not be surprised that his goal for a corn crop will be unfulfilled. He may be angry and upset, but the outcome is simply a natural result, a promise, coming from a fundamental truth (that seeds bear fruit after their own kind) encompassed by the principle.

Although the principle "you reap what you sow" can be seen as merely a restatement of the truth about seeds, it has within its statement an implicit suggestion about how to act based on that truth. The principle is a beginning, cause, source, or a motivation for action. We will do something or not based on the principle. The principle wraps the truth in active terms.

To understand the impact of principles in our lives, then, we must recognize that we believe some things are true and others are not. We value some things over others because they are more valuable guides to the kinds of results we are looking for. And we recognize that our *belief* in the truthfulness of some things is not the measuring rod, the reason, or the final arbiter of whether some things are true or not. There are truths that are truth whether or not we believe in them. Seeds bear fruit after their own kind is naturally true. We can modify seeds to create a modified plant, but that does not alter the fundamental truths that the seeds planted yield the intended, corresponding plants. What of spontaneous variation and mutations in plants? I do not know enough about seeds to give much of an answer, but I can say that whatever the plant is that grows came from the seed it came from. And mutation and variation do not contradict that fundamental idea.

We see that truth is independent in its sphere. Truth is not dependent on our knowing it or on our creating it. But certainly we bring our perceptions and capacities to the truths we encounter. When we do so, we adopt and we often adapt the truths to make sense for us. We accept some truths, we reject other truths, and we alter some truths as well. Thus we engage in meaning making for ourselves. We try to make sense of things and people and events. And we may not always be able to accept or understand (morally or intellectually) truth, but we certainly find some truths to live by. And because we adapt and alter truths often to fit our circumstances and capacities, the truths we live by may not always be true. But we do act *as if* they are true, and we develop or accept principles wrapped around those acceptable-to-us truths.

Of course, principles based on true truths yield consistent and correlated results and outcomes. The promises of the principles come true. Principles based on altered truth (or what seems to be true to us right now, but may not really be true) may yield inconsistent or unintended results. The promises are less certain. Our action based on the principle is no less certain, but the results are unexpected. Furthermore, those unexpected results are basically the outcome of untrue principles. For instance, if we desire a cohesive, unified group of employees, we may not achieve that result if we follow a principle that states competition yields productivity. Competition simply may not yield group cohesion and unity if some of the group is competing with other parts of the group. The subgroups individually may feel united, but not the whole. Competition may yield efficiency, productivity, or a sense of pride in some but not others. But competition may not yield naturally a sense of cohesion and togetherness among everyone involved. No wonder a hypothetical manager who uses competition as a motivator in the office may feel frustrated that people are not always friendly with each other, and concerned with a palpable lack of esprit de corps. She may believe competition always yields cohesiveness, but that doesn't make it necessarily true. To reiterate, though, that manager acts *as if* the principle is true because it is true to the manager. And that manager may always be resigned to be frustrated at her inability to bring people together.

We all have principles we act upon. Some of the principles we act upon that are not true may act upon us as well. They may limit our choices to act, because the results of the less-than-true principles are not what we expected, and so we are left to wonder and to hesitate and to worry. We become reactive in trying to resolve the unintended results. We are thus unable to be proactive in the work we do. A *reactive* stance is one where the circumstances act upon us. A *proactive* stance is where we act upon circumstance; where we are able to always act because the results are what we expected because they are natural results of the truth found in the principle that grounded our action.

What can an understanding of principles do to help us understand values and leadership? We can see that people engage in leadership based on their beliefs about what kinds of actions will yield certain results. Either implicitly or explicitly, these people who do leadership have principles of leadership they have adopted that guide their behaviors, beliefs, mindsets, tools, and so forth in their leadership efforts. They may not be aware of them, but they are there. Uncovering the principles grounding their action (and the reasons for their actions) tells us something about their leadership (or at least their view of it). Aggregating such leadership principles should tell us something about leadership. The challenge is that not everyone may do leadership the same. They may base their leadership on different principles. In fact, it is reasonable to suggest that it is possible that some principles that people use to do leadership may be contradictory or opposite. Therefore it is necessary not only to determine the principles of leadership but also to determine their relative merit and efficacy.

In any case, leadership is a principled-based activity where principle is defined as a way of making sense of certain values and the results of living by those values. Values become practical and operationalized, and their usefulness can be adjudged. Their morality can be similarly adjudged. To do leadership, then, is to live by and promote values, made real by principles, which are consistent with the results the leader wishes and that yield results that can be judged moral or not.

Points to Ponder

1. What does "messing with people's values" mean to you? Do you think it is possible to mess with someone else's values?
2. What is valuable to you? Why? Is it easier to determine what is not a value for you rather than what is? Why or why not?

3. How do you handle manipulators that enter your life? Have you ever engaged in covert aggression to get what you wanted? If yes, how successful were you? Did you "feel good" about it?
4. Why is open and honest choice essential to leadership?
5. Are you aware of your values sets enough that you could influence others to adopt the same or similar values rankings?
6. What are some of the ways values are adopted by people? In other words, how could you teach someone to adopt certain values instead of other values?
7. What can people in positions of authority do to impact the values of the group?
8. What do you think is the power of principles? Is living and leading by principles a realistic notion in today's society? Why or why not?
9. Do you feel comfortable with the idea of leading others based on your values and the values of other people?

Quotables

1. "When your values are clear to you, making decisions becomes easier." —Roy Disney, businessman
2. "The greatest danger for most of us is not that our aim is too high and we miss it, but that it is too low and we reach it." —Michelangelo
3. "Determine that the thing can and shall be done and then we shall find the way." —Abraham Lincoln
4. "Be as you wish to seem." —Socrates

Practical Activities

1. *Identify Your Values.* Identifying your values is a key element of leadership. Often it is a difficult introspective process to list out and "own" your values. And you may miss a few. Another way to identify your values, or at least validate your own list, is to have others do it for you. Ask a close friend (or one not so close, if you like) to list what he or she thinks are your values—the values you live by and the values you aspire to. Not knowing your inner voice, this friend will usually make such judgments based on your words and behavior and on how your words and behavior align. They may see things in your daily living that you gloss over or choose to downplay. Such second-hand verification of your values is a powerful way to ensure that your depiction of your values set is in line with how you live. It may serve as a starting point for personal growth and introspection as well.
2. *Choosing Organizational Values.* Identifying the values in play in an organization is the first step toward knowing whether to lead a values change effort

TABLE 2.5. Identifying Your Leadership Principles

Leadership Principle	Action	Result
Go the extra mile.	Seek for and capitalize on opportunities to work with others beyond my own job description.	Increased task accomplishment with relationships of trust and respect growing in the group.

or do things that reinforce the values. It is a central act of leadership to pick the values the organization commits to. Choose an organization with which you are familiar. Make a list of what you think the organization's values are. If there is a published statement or a formal list of the organization's values, then compare your list with the published list. Are there differences? Choose one of the values you would like to "mess with." Specify why the change is necessary and then identify the practical steps you would take to make the new value more evident in the work of the organization.

3. *Identifying Your Leadership Principles.* Knowing what your leadership principles are tells you a lot about what you think leadership is. Sharing your principles with others will allow them more information to use to choose to follow or not. Make a chart with three headings: Principle, Action, and Result. List three or four principles you think are essential to good leadership. Then outline the actions that come from such principles and the results you expect from those actions. Add to the list as you continue to think about your views of leadership. See the example in Table 2.5.

Notes

1. Matthew R. Fairholm and Gilbert W. Fairholm, *Understanding Leadership Perspectives: Theoretical and Practical Approaches* (New York: Springer, 2009), 86.

2. For example, Warren Bennis and Burt Nanus, *Leaders: The Strategies for Taking Charge* (New York: HarperCollins, 1985); John Gardner, *On Leadership* (New York: Free Press, 1990); Jay A. Conger, "Inspiring Others: The Language of Leadership," *Academy of Management Executive* 5 (1991): 31–45; Gilbert W. Fairholm, *Values Leadership: Toward a New Philosophy of Leadership* (New York: Praeger, 1991); Stephen R. Covey, *Principle-Centered Leadership* (New York: Simon and Schuster, 1992); Max DePree, *Leadership Jazz* (New York: Dell, 1992); James O'Toole, *Leading Change: The Argument for Value-Based Leadership* (New York: Ballantine Books, 1996); James Kouzes and Barry Posner, *The Leadership Challenge: How to Get Extraordinary Things Done in Organizations*, 4th ed. (San Francisco: Jossey-Bass, 2008); Gilbert W. Fairholm, *Real Leadership: How Spiritual Values Give Leadership Meaning* (Santa Barbara, CA: Praeger, 2011).

3. "Survey: Employer's, Employees' Core Values Sometimes Don't Coincide," *Chief Learning Officer*, April 16, 2007, http://clomedia.com/articles/view/survey_employer_s_employees_core_values_sometimes_don_t_coincide.

4. Ibid., ¶ 5–9.

5. James M. Burns, *Leadership* (New York: Harper and Row, 1978).

6. Ibid., 11.

7. Matthew R. Fairholm, "The Themes and Theory of Leadership: James MacGregor Burns and Moral Leadership," Center for Excellence in Municipal Management, Washington, DC, 2001, http://www.dccpm.org/scripts/files/leadershipfiles-mattfairholm.php.

8. Ibid., 2.

9. Burns, *Leadership*, 41.

10. Ibid., 18.

11. Ibid., 19.

12. Ibid.

13. Fairholm, "The Themes and Theory of Leadership," 3.

14. Ibid.

15. Burns, *Leadership,* 64.

16. Fairholm, "The Themes and Theory of Leadership," 4.

17. Ibid., italics in the original.

18. Ibid.

19. Gardner, *On Leadership*, 191.

20. Milton Rokeach, *The Nature of Human Values* (New York: Free Press, 1973), 5.

21. Ibid., 48–50.

22. Rushworth M. Kidder, "Universal Human Values: Finding an Ethical Common Ground," *Public Management* 77 (1995): 4–9.

23. Ibid., 6–7.

24. Rokeach, 18.

25. Peter Senge, *The Fifth Discipline: The Art and Practice of the Learning Organization* (New York: Doubleday, 1990), 228.

Chapter 3

Vision: Pictures of Practice

The quick link between Values and Vision in the Four Vs is simply that Vision operationalizes, or puts into practice, Values. Vision is a manifestation of values. Vision makes values real. It informs people about who they really are (or what the organization really is) and what they can become because of who they are.

Vision springs from deeply held values, ideals, and beliefs. Vision says we are us and perhaps, therefore, unlike others; our vision may not be your vision, but it makes us who we are and it guides our work, giving us purpose, meaning, and in some cases, identity. Vision is how the energy of individual passion is directed toward specific goals. Individuals may have visions of their own for sure, but we are mostly talking about visions that bind individuals together—the purpose and meaning that bring individuals together under a common cause, doing work for a reason. Acting, reacting, and interacting with regard to the values one possesses can be viewed as a working definition of the concept of vision. In reality, if the vision of a group (or a company, organization, team, etc.) is congruent with the visions of the individuals within the group, there is greater impact, greater effect, and greater unity within the group.

Painting a Picture of Practice

I have always liked *vision* as the term signifying that element of leadership that explains purpose, meaning, or current and future states of being. I like it because it makes clear that a leader is to paint a picture in the follower's mind, a picture he or she sees with the mind's eye, that helps a follower make sense of the values and practices that are congruent with or make sense in the cause the leader and follower are choosing to be engaged in.

Vision is a term that reminds us that leadership is about helping others see values in action. One writer described vision as a shared image of a desirable future and a "reflection of our fundamental beliefs and assumptions about the world [springing out of our past knowledge, experience, and intuition] and about the direction the organization should take"[1] to reach the desirable. Another description of vision is an emotionally charged, clear, and vivid picture or mental movie of the future. Visions make our ideals more real as we can "see" the result of our beliefs and actions. Vision helps us see who we are and what we can become because of who we are. Rather than being mere abstraction, a vision helps to operationalize values, further refining who we are and what we are all about. For me, vision is about seeing how values are made effective in our lives and why they are important in the first place.

The notion that leaders paint a picture for their followers highlights the artistic nature of leadership, or the craftsmanship involved in leadership, rather than any notion of a science of leadership. As I looked further into the term *vision*, I realized that my simplistic reading of *vision* was insufficient. True, vision is about seeing. We use the term to describe the effect of one of the senses called sight (as distinguished from smell or touch, for instance). However, the sense of physical sight hasn't always been associated with our modern understanding of the word *vision*. In fact, it wasn't until the fifteenth century that vision acquired this sense.

Before the fifteenth century, *vision* was a word used to describe something seen in the imagination or in the supernatural. It came from old French and Latin root words that indicated the ability to know clearly, or to see without darkness. To have vision was to know; it was to see as the wise see. This early reading of the term *vision* adds depth and meaning to the leader's activity of painting a picture of values in action in the minds of followers. Leaders use vision to help us know things in ways we didn't know before and to give us clarity about who we are and what we are all about. The leadership element of vision asks us to be able to see not only with our head but with our heart as well. It makes sense, but it also feels right; and it is from that combination that a follower makes the choice to follow (and that a leader makes the choice to lead).

A Word on Vision Statements

A vision is more than merely a statement of some future state of affairs. A vision isn't really a statement at all. It is a picture that paints truth in action for the group that adopts it. It is grounded in certain values and is understood by both head and heart.

But this is not what is often taught about visions. Instead, a vision is said to be a statement of purpose with a future orientation. We reduce the power of a picture (which is worth a thousand words) to a vision statement of only a few words. I have been in training sessions where I was told a vision statement should be no more than eight words long. Instead of a leader crafting and illustrating a vision for the people, the leader is asked to merely create a statement of purpose, essentially a bumper sticker. In this sense, to have a vision is merely to have a vision statement. It diminishes the potential power of a vision and in some ways limits what leader and follower can see and act on in the vision. In this vein, visions are merely known as vision statements, and something is lost in the reduction.

People often disregard vision statements as a wordsmithing exercise, a task for a leader to accomplish rather than a values-based picture of truth a leader lives by. I remember when President George H. W. Bush, during the 1988 presidential campaign, created controversy when he referred to the "vision thing" in a somewhat offhanded and disparaging way. The comment elicited disagreements about a leader's ability to forge the future or to merely make incremental impacts at best.[2] But who could blame him when the invigorating element of vision is reduced by consultants and management fads to a statement we create at executive retreats and post in corporate hallways? The phrases within vision statements often feel as if they were checked out of some vision statement warehouse wherein are shelves filled with terms like "world-class," "customer service," "industry leader," "best in class," and the like that have come to be cliché and bereft of meaning because of overuse.

I hope I don't give the wrong impression. Vision statements are a useful tool, but the statement is not the leadership element. The vision statement is a way to shorthand the grand vision picture that energizes people to work together, to be united, and to be one with others. A good vision statement reflects core purposes of the organization or the leader (or both) and articulates a feasible, even if challenging, result that has significance beyond the immediate goal. Vision statements are horizon ideas that change the relationship among team members and provide a common purpose. They represent the raison d'être for the group's activities and serve as a standard of reaching decisions and directing activities. When people hear or read the statement, they are reminded of the picture, sparking the imagination and touching the head and the heart. It should remind us of the values at play and how to put those values into practice every day.

There is an example of a statement I personally like. It has the potential to do just what a statement ought to do: wrap the values into a compelling picture that affects how we view ourselves, others, and the work we engage in. This example comes from the Ritz Carlton Hotels. The Ritz calls it their motto or gold standard, but it seems to fit the notion of a vision statement. It goes like this: "We are Ladies and Gentlemen serving Ladies and Gentlemen."

Notice how this statement seems to do at least two things at the same time. First, it translates their corporate values into a picture of the type of people the employees are and/or ought to be. Second, it implies some picture of activity, and a standard of activity, that they undertake day to day. I also find it interesting that the statement is not necessarily forward thinking. It doesn't imply that "in the next 20 years we will be the world-class hospitality company of choice for business and leisure guests." Their motto is current. It tells me who they are (who I am if I worked there). But it is at the same time aspirational and future oriented. It tells me as a Ritz worker who I ought to be (and can be) because of who I am. No matter what I was like before, as a Ritz Carlton employee, I am a service-oriented gentleman (or I am ever striving to be one).

This vision statement works in the hospitality business. The values at play and the goals intended are specific to the industry. Certainly, not every endeavor can simply steal that motto to its benefit. And not every leader may share those same values. The endeavor, and the values, and the industry vary, but vision statements bring people together under a picture of practice. The best vision statements get personal (even if they are advocated in corporations and organizations) and help me know what we (in the collective activity) are all about, what we are like, and what we ought to be doing to be more like that. The best vision statements point to a state of being that puts into practice the values we believe in or are coming to believe in and helps me apply those values in the work we have decided to do together.

How to Have a Vision

For a vision to be compelling to others, it has to be compelling to the leader. Perhaps like me, you have been involved in retreats (or can imagine this scenario playing out) where organization members get together to craft the organization's vision. Through some group process, ideas are floated and then maybe voted on until a short list of general themes emerges, some of which are then wrapped into a wordsmithed statement: the vision. I have often found that the figurehead leader is frequently not involved in this process very much, usually offering the excuse that he or she wants to hear from others and doesn't want to spoil the process or poison the well, so to speak. This lack of involvement is, of course, a supposed show of openness and desire to listen.

What emerges, therefore, often has no relevance (or even input) to what the leader-in-title desires or feels about the group. We have already touched on some of the limitations of the vision statement as opposed to a vision, but this process highlights them even more. Often this vision retreat is in all practicality led by a member or two who do have passion about some element or other of the organization and are able to influence the group (i.e., lead the group) into adopting such principles and values they deem important to be included in the ultimate vision statement.

Imagine after the retreat, however, that the figurehead leader returns to work still neither interested nor invested in the new vision. It wasn't his vision anyway, as he kept his mouth shut. It was, in fact, the vision of a few people exerting leadership during the retreat.

Some results are inevitable. The figurehead leader does not walk the talk. Certainly he approved new logos, new signs, even new training around the vision. But it is a show. It is another program, in his mind, that needs to be managed well. But he has no passion for it and often runs things counter to the vision he officially espouses. Followers grow frustrated. The figurehead gets frustrated. Inconsistencies, confusion, disappointment, and misunderstandings occur.

Another result is often inevitable. The leaders of the new vision—the one or two people who drove the retreat and influenced the group members to adopt the new vision—become a second option of loyalty within the organization, especially for those who attended the retreat. Rather than increased respect, loyalty, and collaboration, there is a power struggle with the "real" leaders of the organization and the figurehead leader. That power struggle is really a struggle of values and vision, even a culture clash. Since the unveiling of the new vision, the "vision leaders" became de facto leaders to all the organization members who agreed with and adopted the vision in the work they do. They hence become frustrated and suspicious of the figurehead who was supposed to agree with the vision at the retreat but never did anything congruent with it. These members are loyal to the exemplars of the vision; they are not loyal to the figurehead.

I think the point is made. Virus-like office politics result, as do many organizational difficulties that are the subjects of innumerable books.

People suffer, the organization suffers, the products or services provided suffer, and the need for new vision or new formal leadership is felt all over. All of this is the result mainly of that figurehead not being the leader, not being the visionary. It highlights the fact that leaders are not always at the top; that position is not the essential nature of leadership. It highlights too that if one is at the top, that person is a leader only if he or she does things leaders do, like set and share vision.

Implicit in this talk of vision is that a leader's personal values and personal outlook impact the overall vision of the group of followers. The leader is important in the vision process mainly because the leader's values drive the vision. Two issues emerge. First, how does a leader get a vision in the first place? Second, how involved are followers in developing the leader's vision? Tackling the first issue involves at least three elements: knowing yourself, knowing others, and knowing where your values should take you.

Know Yourself

To set a vision, leaders have to first *want* to set a vision and then know what they really believe in. Otherwise, no one else will believe in it either. Knowing ourselves is essential. Getting straight in our minds what our values are is essential. Knowing how those values are related to the work being done or the work wanting to be done within a group is essential too. A compelling vision for others is first compelling to the leader.

I discuss the concept of gaining a sense of self further in chapter 5. But here it is important to mention that self-awareness is essential to leadership. So is a sense of how leaders interact with others. A number of personality and behavioral assessments can be used to help with this self-awareness, and many of them can be found online. But more than these diagnostics, we must be aware of what we stand for and why. We need to be aware of how we fit and associate with others. Some of this insight can be gained from the research on emotional intelligence. Some can be found through introspection and personal reflection.

Research on emotional intelligence emerged through studies about why ostensibly intelligent people fail to be successful.[3] Leadership authors Richard Hughes, Robert Ginnett, and Gordon Curphy offer a definition of emotional intelligence as a "set of mental abilities that help people recognize their own feelings and those of others"[4] and conclude that "leaders who can better align their thoughts and feelings with their actions are more effective than leaders who think and feel one way about something but then do something different about it."[5] These abilities are refined differently by different people and make up a sense of their overall emotional capacities. Examples of these abilities include self-regulation, empathy, self-awareness, social skills, a facility with sources and types of personal motivation, and the like.

Personal reflection is an activity many people avoid. It requires some sense of humility to engage in introspection and self-assessment. It can be even harder to do as we focus on working and getting things done. I am learning, though, that reflecting on tasks while engaged in them is a critical skill to develop for successful leadership.

Building on the theories of learning as transformation, it becomes clear that reflection is an integral part of both learning and personal transformation.[6] Simply put, we do something and then we reflect or ask questions about it. However, there are different levels of reflection that reveal different insights: the deeper the reflection, the deeper the insights and the more profound learning taking place. Figure 3.1 illustrates the kinds of reflection we might engage in, and the enhanced learning about ourselves and the situations each succeeding level of reflection offers us. The first is the Incidental Reflection, where we simply review the activity and immediate result. For instance, I could reflect on the work of balancing a budget. A reflection on the incident could

FIGURE 3.1. Reflection Learning Model

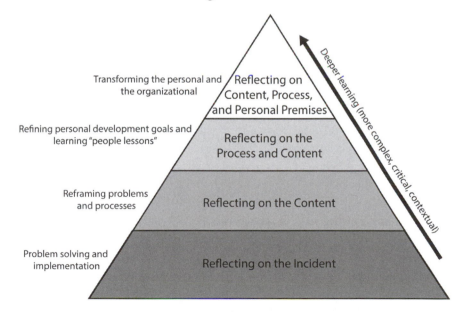

take the form "it was fun," or "we made it through," or "it was miserable," or "we couldn't balance it," or "they wouldn't give in on their position." All of these reflection statements are useful to a degree, but if I stay at this level, I won't do much learning about myself or much evaluating of the situation and my place in it. And I may remain a rather mediocre budget person.

If my goal is to have deeper, more complex insights and learning about myself and how I interact with people and the work at hand, I need to start moving up the triangle of reflection. The next level is the Content Reflection stage. At this level, I begin to look at what the problem or work included, rather than merely the outcome or incident. I begin to consider the decisions made that caused one element to be in the budget or another not to be included. I begin to reflect on what was left in and what was left out and why. Such reflection helps me reframe questions and problems and in the process helps me know what is important and what is not.

Still further up the triangle, I can engage in the Process and Content Reflection. This stage helps me analyze not just what was in or out of the budget, but why. I begin to see internal processes and the interactions with other people and evaluate what criteria were important, what procedures were in place, what personalities helped or hindered, and why. I begin to reflect on what I negotiated and what the negotiations looked like. I can analyze how well I did within the process, and I can evaluate other people and their interactions with me. This level moves me beyond the incident and takes my reflection to my own work, into my own interactions with others and into my own developmental goals.

Still deeper and more complex learning about me occurs at the Process, Premise, and Content Reflection stage. This I call my values-and-principles-reflection stage. This is the level that offers me the deepest and most complex insights into myself and my interactions. At this level, I begin to ask myself questions about whether I liked the processes or how I felt during the process. I might take specific situations and reflect on why I couldn't work in that group, or why that person frustrates me so much, or how confused I get when such and such happens. I begin to look inward to see how I impact the outward. I begin to look inward to see how I impact other things and people.

Learning to reflect while we do the work allows us to gauge ourselves and become more aware. It allows us to change and evolve and improve. It allows us to learn about ourselves, deeply. Such learning makes us better able to influence and lead others. With that reflection, then, I am in a better position to know who I am, what my values are, and the kind of work to be engaged in. If I do this often, I create better visions. I become a reflective practitioner and a wiser leader.

The benefit of such reflection is continuous learning. The more I am able to improve my work due to reflecting on that very work itself, the more productive and relevant I am in the collective activity. But more than that, the more I reflect and learn about myself, the better able I am to explain values and paint vision pictures for others to understand. As I learn continually and reflect on work, interactions of people, and my own progress and growth I gain wisdom and refinement in painting pictures of practice for others. I create better visions and more compelling reasons for others to follow me.

Know Others

Vision creation is not an act performed in isolation. When a leader chooses to encourage a vision for others to adopt, the leader must take into account the "others." Leaders must have some connection with and understanding of the potential community they are trying to influence. The values of others must be close enough to the values in the leader's vision for the vision to be compelling. Otherwise, the potential followers will be in a state of values confusion (or at least have a lukewarm commitment to a set of values) and will be looking for the values that the leader's vision encompasses. Leaders need to be aware of the followers' environment to make sure that their vision has the potential of ever being adopted by the people they hope to influence. Certainly, there is work involved in sharing a vision, but there must be some confidence in the mind of the leader that his or her work of influence actually has a chance. Leaders need to know others.

To know others is a daunting task. It asks leaders to discern, to be wise, to be astute, and in some ways to be lucky in their guesses about people. But the risk can be minimized by learning about the history, the sociology, and the generally accepted cultures of the group. Leaders can scan the environment in preparation for the messages and vision that is both needed and might be accepted by the group.

An example from Shakespeare's *Henry V* may be helpful in illustrating the point of scanning and evaluating the followers' condition. In Act 4, Scene 3, the play presents the famous St. Crispin's Day speech in preparation for a mighty battle with the French. But it is Scene 1 of the same act that captures my attention as well. We find King Henry disguising himself as he walks throughout the camp, interacting with the soldiers. He asks questions, he listens, he argues, he gets a feel for what the soldiers are thinking about—and more importantly feeling—on the eve of what promises to be a difficult battle against overwhelming odds. To make a long story short (and of course, you should think about reading the play), it was Henry's scanning of the encampment, his interactions with the soldiers, and his personal struggles with the issues at hand that help him shape the message, the stories, and the ultimate vision communicated in the St. Crispin's Day speech. He got to know the men. Certainly, his own filters and perceptions, biases, hopes, and dreams flavored his interpretations of the environmental scan, but that is the case with us all. We do our best and make the effort to know the others we wish to influence. But with that effort, our visions (and how we present those visions) become that much more palatable to potential followers and appropriate to the situation.

Some Useful Tools for Figuring People Out

When scanning the environment and trying to get to know others, I find it useful to adapt some ideas from anthropology and archaeology. Both disciplines try to discern the cultures and practices of different groups of people by examining bits and pieces of evidence. They get to know the culture and the people by looking at what they do or leave behind or think about or use day to day. We too can adapt the methodologies of those disciplines to help us figure people out. Table 3.1 summarizes these helpful hints.

The first helpful pieces of evidence are artifacts and symbols that people use or leave behind. These are things that are important to them and are represented in the things they use, the art they admire, the objects or people they revere, and the like. One colleague taught me that one of the

TABLE 3.1 Figuring People Out or What Gives People Away

Artifacts and Symbols	Objects or physical representations of the group culture (e.g., art, language, flags, clothing, technology)
Stories and Myths	Verbal representations (fact and fiction) that emphasize critical values and explain beliefs of the culture
Relationships	Formal and informal linkages between people (e.g., titles and organizational structures, temporary alliances, individual interactions, hierarchy, social norms)
Rituals and Rules of Behavior	Formal things (e.g., policies, practices, written and sanctioned ceremonies) and informal things (e.g., emergent norms, ad hoc awards, "the way things are done around here") that people typically do

best things to look for to figure someone out is the person's computer screensaver. Is it the company logo? The last family picture? The mascot of a favorite sports team? The last vacation photos? Similar artifacts can be found, too, by looking at the little knickknacks around the office. What's on the walls? What kinds of pictures are framed on the desk, if any? What kinds of technology are found in the office? What type of furniture is used? What is on the office doors? Are there names on them? Do they use titles? In the office, do people address each other on a first-name basis or use more formal interactions? These pieces of information help a leader discern what is important to people individually and to the group as a whole.

Stories and myths are other great resources for leaders to use to figure people out. We will talk later of the power of stories. No doubt we learn a lot about people from the stories they create or disseminate. Office myths are powerful, whether true or not, and reveal what occupies people's minds. How people speak to each other and what they talk about are powerful indicators of their values, their worries, and their focus—in short, their culture.

The order and structure and type of relationships that exist in the group and among people also help us figure people out. Are relationships formal or informal? Are they permanent or temporary? Do certain people hang out with only certain other people? What is the reason? Do individuals have a say, or is dissent discouraged? What is done with the rebel? How are "go-to people" chosen? What rewards or punishments are there? These characteristics of people's interactions help us know what makes people tick.

The last of the tricks of the trade is to analyze the rituals and rules of behavior that exist in a group or are carried out by individuals. Do people clock in? Is there a set time for lunch? Is being late tolerated? There are formal and informal rituals. Some are written down as standard operating procedures, but many are below the surface. Like an iceberg where up to 90 percent of the mass is underwater and unseen, the informal or unwritten rules have a major impact on people and groups. Is there an unwritten rule about how fast employees work? Is there pressure to do things *this* way even if the rules say to do them *that* way? Are there steps to follow? Knowing "the way things work around here," especially if they don't work according to standard operating procedures, is a powerful indicator of the values and culture of a group.

Every One and Everyone

Getting to know others is, in many ways, a skill consciously exercised. The benefit is that values and vision are more accurately discerned, developed, and disseminated when we know each other. Obviously, in large-scale organizations, it may not be possible to know everyone individually. We may have to rely on knowing the general makeup of the group. Therefore two sets of skills are needed for leaders: knowing every *one* (individual characteristics and concerns) and knowing *everyone* (large group characteristics and concerns). Both sets of skills require one thing: information.

As leaders, we do have a core group of people we interact with routinely. That sphere of influence is relatively small but allows for far more personal relationships. The information we gather from this group is more detailed and person-specific. With this group of people, we need to develop the interpersonal trust and interactions to get to personalities, preferences, personal goals, and premises about life and the world we live in. I have learned that much of the leader's job is to lower other people's sense of caution about people and things.

When people are less cautious they are more trusting and more willing to interact genuinely. This is not possible without interacting. Face-to-face interactions are important. Meetings are more than mere exchanges of strategic or tactical information about the group's goals. They can serve to be a way of getting to know each other too. Leaders find ways to interact with individuals so that there is mutual understanding and a relationship based on more than mere business transactions. These interactions help us know every *one* person we influence and help that person influence us as well.

I remember the story of a coffee shop manager that may help us see what the focus on the *one* might look like. By day, the manager was in charge of a coffee shop, and by night she was a member of a punk band. She really liked the people she worked with, including a particular employee we'll name Bob. Bob was not very good at making coffee—he was messy and slow, and his drinks weren't a hit with the customers. The manager was concerned because the company required routine evaluations of its employees' abilities to make drinks properly and maintain cleanliness. Interestingly, the manager put it this way: "Unfortunately, for everyone, the company did evaluations." It was everyone's problem, in her view, that *one* employee might not meet the standards. Everyone else was doing just fine; only Bob had the problem. But to this manager, it was everyone's problem that not every *one* of them would pass. Bob mattered.

The manager weighed her options: she could fire Bob or work twice as hard (and include other people in the effort) to make sure Bob passed the evaluation. She realized her sacrifice for the one would cause others to pick up the slack and, on a personal note, she would have to miss some punk shows. She made her decision. She talked it over with her punk band, and as she put it, "they all understood, because they had day jobs working for the man too." She was going to take care of the one and recruited the rest of the crowd to help in the process. She didn't believe in firing people and, as she put it, she cared about Bob.

This manager worked nights and days with Bob, "biting her nails" along the way. She recited fun though perhaps exaggerated comments about the experience, like "Bob, that is a sponge, not a lemon tart!" or "Bob, the bleach is used for cleaning. It's not a substitute for vanilla flavoring!" or "Oh dear, Bob, the toaster is on fire again!" However, it turned out that she had no need to worry. On the day of evaluations, Bob was neat and clean, moved like never before, and made drinks quickly, properly, and that actually tasted good. This manager, remembering that everyone includes every *one*, said, "Everyone passed the evaluations with flying colors" and afterward, "the kids in the café took Bob to his favorite restaurant."

Who can argue about this manager's concern for Bob; she put the *one* in everyone. It required sacrifice, time, worry, and a real sense of caring for Bob as a person. Leadership recognizes that everyone includes every *one*. Through her example, this barista showed us what that looks like. We can only imagine what impact her focus on the one had on Bob and the rest of the employees in that café. I can picture great reservoirs of trust, caring, and commitment that the group could draw upon as they worked together.

Nevertheless, leaders also need to see the forest, not only the trees; they have to see *everyone* as well as every *one*. Different from knowing every one, the skill of knowing everyone requires different activities. Certainly trying to interact with everyone is a noble goal, but depending upon the size and scope of the organization, it may be impractical.

We still need information about the people though. This information is different from the more personal information and focus described above, but it is still descriptive of people in the group. Surveys, suggestions boxes, open-door policies, meet-and-greet sessions, and the like are all ways of gaining information about the people in the group. So too are certain performance metrics of the organization. Furthermore, much information can be gained about others in the groups by tapping into the grapevine. Figuring out what is on people's minds and what is being floated informally in the organization is extremely helpful. A leader cannot be so isolated from individuals that he or she is oblivious to the informal concerns and issues being discussed in the lunchroom or by the water cooler.

In some sense, that is what King Henry did in Shakespeare's play. First, he knew his intimate group well. He was aware of the likes and dislikes, personalities, and concerns of his inner circle. Second, he was concerned enough about his larger group of people to enter into conversations, discern their concerns, and listen—just listen—to people talk. Leaders need to know others. They need to gain information about people individually and people in groups.

Although the kinds of information needed about every *one* and about *everyone* are different, the desire to garner such information and engage with it is constant. The benefits accrue as we engender trust, gain wisdom, evaluate personal and group values, and begin to craft and communicate both Vision and Vector (see chapter 4). Getting to know others is also a way to remind leaders to support and encourage Voice (see chapter 5) among those being led.

Knowing Where Your Values Should Take You

As visions are so intimately connected with the values that undergird them, a leader needs to know where the values naturally lead—that is, which behaviors and mind-sets the values naturally intend. In this way the vision is expressed in ways consistent with the value principle. The vision is congruent with the promise each value holds in terms of current and future states of being and activities taken. Leaders must know where the values should take us.

Much of this was discussed earlier in chapter 2 on values when we discussed the power of principles with promise. To summarize here, leaders need to remember that values are not isolated. In other words, values live within the person but also have results that live on outside of the person. There is direction and morality to values, and living by some values and not others will shape lives differently. Living by values has results. We all live by values and reap the consequences.

Leaders recognize that the values they choose intend a certain kind of outcome. Yes, there are variations around the theme of the values we live by, but there is in fact a theme. There is a general direction, morality, or result that is associated with values. Leaders know this and choose some values over others upon which to lead because those values will generally help the leader get to where (and how) the leader wants to go (and in what way).

Visions Are Leader-Centric, but Follower-Focused

Tackling the second issue raised above—"How involved are followers in developing the leader's vision?"—we have to remember that people who lead *themselves* only are not doing leadership in the way we are talking about. Leading oneself is an important element of the leadership phenomenon, and we have already talked about knowing ourselves. But as we deal with the subject in this discussion, we acknowledge that leadership is about a relationship. It involves multiple people. It is about followers as much as or more than it is about the leader. We accept that leaders create vision. It is a leader-centric activity related to the leader's own values and applied to specific situations and groups. However, a leader-centric vision in isolation is often neither inspiring nor compelling.

Followers adopting a leader's vision—a leader's description of certain values in action in certain ways—is almost the defining element of the overall notion of leadership. Without followers, there is no leader. Followers follow one leader and not another because of the vision that leader outlines and exemplifies. Such vision operationalizes values that the followers like or want to like. Accordingly, leader visions are necessarily linked to other people. Visions are the responsibility of the leader but are focused on (and shaped a little by) the follower as well.

In this sense, a leader-led but follower-focused vision does two things. It grounds the leader and it inspires the followers. Visions do as much to remind the leader of what is important and what his or her efforts are all about as it encourages the followers to learn what is important and what their efforts should be about. A well-crafted, values-driven vision makes sure the leader doesn't forget why he or she chose to lead in the first place and to what end that leadership takes people. Such a reminder is often needed in times of struggle and disappointment. A leader can rely on the vision to reinvigorate her or him when times are tough. A vision can help a leader remember what is really important and what past efforts were intended to do.

Furthermore, a vision can inspire the followers and remind them why they are engaged in the work together. The investments a follower makes to a leader and to a leader's vision can be substantial. On the other hand, as Peter Senge, author of *The Fifth Discipline*, stated, "A vision not consistent with values that people live by day to day will not only fail to inspire enthusiasm, it will also foster outright cynicism."[7]

For example, a sales director who preaches the vision of respect for others and concern for the employees who then, in a sales team meeting, publicly shames and denigrates an employee or two who have not met sales expectations for the month is being inconsistent, even hypocritical. The sales director will end up with employees who are working only out of fear of public shame and reprimand and who neither believe in nor trust the leader due to his or her lack of integrity and commitment to the vision and values. Workers invest in the vision, and leaders should too.

Such intellectual, emotional, and talent-based investments often cause followers to want a reminder of why this is all worth it. Vision does that. It reminds us of why and how day-to-day activity is linked to an overall purpose and meaning. The story of the Chinese Bank division in the previous chapter is an example of a senior manager instilling in the division supervisor and staff a new vision of both themselves as workers and of the work itself. Another example also highlights what buying into the vision can do for us and for our organizations.

A large, Midwest-based nonprofit organization dealing with juvenile participants in the criminal justice system has focused on its vision for years—and both the organization and its vision have lasted beyond its founder. That element of the story is really striking and speaks to the power of the vision and the commitment of the organization and the people in it to the vision. The organization started as a small outfit processing the intake and disposition of juveniles in the court system. But the vision of the leader and her actions corresponding to it were too much to ignore or overlook. It was contagious. The vision was wrapped around these core ideas: rebuilding lives, strengthening communities, and restoring hope. Before long, grant money started coming in, new staff members who were committed to the cause were hired, and eventually this small nonprofit organization grew into a major policy player in the field with millions of dollars in operating budget.

The vision was powerful and attracted people to it. The people stayed true to the cause, because they believed in it, and the organization acted congruently with it. When the founder finally backed away from positional, day-to-day responsibilities, the new management didn't miss a step. Today, the organization has weathered the good and the bad economic times, is still a policy player, and provides the kinds of services it always intended to provide. The power of the vision—rebuilding lives, strengthening communities, and restoring hope—and the people's commitment to it has lasted through transition, economic distress, and the emotional ups and downs that are a part of the work they do.

Vision is essentially a process of infusing people's lives with a greater purpose. An organizational vision can provide guidance to the whole, but to be the most effective, the vision has to be felt and developed at a personal level. Certainly, a vision grounds the leader while at the same time it inspires the followers.

A Word on Inspiration

This thing called *inspiration* is a tricky one to define sometimes. Often inspiration is coupled with its cousin *motivation*. In doing so, people often think they are the same thing. They aren't. Motivation is an extremely useful idea in organizations, but it doesn't have quite the leadership implications that inspiration does. In fact, motivation has more to do with management. This is because motivation is about getting others to move, to have others do something wanted done by someone else. Basically, motivation is merely the application of incentives and, as such, loses its usefulness to leaders as we begin to understand what leadership really is.

There is a real business case to be made to clarify what motivation and inspiration are and then determine how to do either one of them. Leadership authors Hughes, Ginnett, and Curphy cite a Gallup poll taken in 2000 that estimates "that if companies could get 3.7 percent more work out of each employee, the equivalent of 18 more minutes of work for each eight-hour shift, the gross domestic product in the U.S. would swell by $355 billion."[8] Furthermore, they suggest that "people believed they could give as much as 15 percent or 20 percent more effort at work than they now do with *no one*, including their own bosses, recognizing any difference."[9] So motivating others, or perhaps inspiring them, is important to organizations and perhaps is an essential element of leaders interacting with followers.

The French root of the word *motivation* has to do with motion and movement. Motivation occurs as one gets others to do things the motivator wants done and that the people see personal benefit in doing. To motivate others, one taps into the fulfillment of their needs, or explains and creates rational processes that cause others to agree with goals of motivation, or trains people in such a way that they naturally and intuitively move.

The bottom line here is that we are getting others to do what we want them to do. We act upon them. We can even help them to like whatever it is we want them to do or even to desire to do it themselves. But it is our goal, our need, and our behavior we want from them that is the key. Our efforts and needs are the motivator, the source of motion. In some odd way, when we motivate others it is only because we feel some motive to have them do something; in other words, it is more about our motivation than it is theirs.

A textbook definition says that we know motivation is happening when three things are present: intensity, direction, and persistence. Figure 3.2 shows how the three elements may interact. *Intensity* is the amount of

FIGURE 3.2. Example of How Motivation Elements Interact to Achieve a Manager's Goal

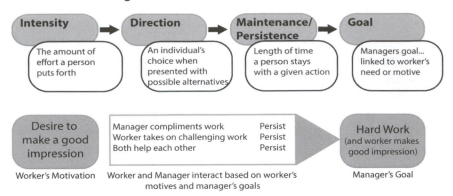

effort a person puts forth. *Direction* is the defined by the individual's choice when presented with a number of alternatives. The person can go this way or that. If he goes in the proper direction (the one the manager wants), we call the person motivated. *Persistence* is the length of time a person stays with a given action.

When the manager has a goal, like getting an employee to work hard, she taps into the motives and needs of an employee. For instance, let's say that an employee wants to make a good impression so that he is considered for a promotion. The manager will interact with that employee to reinforce in the person the feeling that a good impression is being made. One thing she may do is compliment the work being done or allow the employee to take on more challenging work or do favors for the employee. These kinds of things will hopefully cause the employee to persist in his hard work because he has reaped some useful rewards. When all is said and done, all the efforts of employee and manager culminate in a hardworking employee who, over time, impresses the managers. Such an employee is called motivated, and the manager is said to be pretty good.

Inspiration is a little different. The word derives from Latin with the idea of having the spirit (of something, some idea, some cause, and so forth) dwell within someone in such a way that the person finds inner desires to be or do something specific. It means to animate with an idea or purpose, to breathe into a person that which causes inner drives and commitments to shape and enable people to act on their own toward certain hopes or end states.

Rather than external forces being placed on me or trying to convince me of moving in some way, inspiration relies on internal forces that I have that

FIGURE 3.3. The Impact of a Leader's Influence on a Person's Values

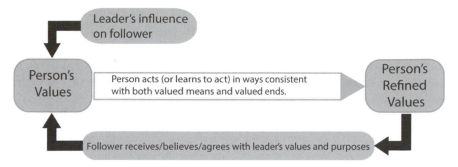

cause me to move. Motivation acts upon me to move; inspiration allows me, even gives me, the inner drive to move in certain directions and in certain ways. In this sense, inspiration taps not into needs but into aspirational wants and beliefs (including values and principles), hopes, and dreams to change the people sufficiently so that they move on their own without external forces or reminders. Inspiration causes people to choose a new way of approaching things (see Figure 3.3). Inspiration is something leaders do *with* a person, not *to* a person; in a very real sense, it is something that occurs *within* the person.

A gymnastics coach in a small town learned what inspiration can do for others, for the one, and for the community at large. She speaks of one girl on her team who had a hard time it seemed with everything (family, school, athletics, and the like). The coach admitted the first month of the season was hard because she had to deal with the poor attitude and inconsistent commitment of the girl. However, by the final two months of the season, the gymnast had turned things around. How? Though the coach hadn't characterized it this way, the truth is the coach was inspired to inspire this gymnast to change.

The coach said that in her mind, the most important thing she did for "Sally" was to help her change her attitude toward life. What a statement. Her techniques were apparently very simple. The coach listened, asked questions, and offered a few answers. She taught Sally how to frame and reframe scenarios to better understand what was going on and to discern possible responses to situations, responses that were otherwise unknown to Sally. Because of the practice schedule, the coach was with Sally a lot. And because Sally always had problems at school, at home, and with others, the coach was in a position to help her learn how to deal with those problems. Even after the gymnastics season ended, Sally still thanked her coach not only for making her a better gymnast but also for helping her become a better person. This kind of focus on the whole person, not just the athlete, is not uncommon among the best coaches around.

Apparently, Sally was not the only one inspired by this coach. When pushed to share, the coach admitted that, because of her coaching, more people in the community recognized her on the streets for shaping what they called her "little gymnasts." In addition to their parents, the teachers, friends, brothers and sisters, grandparents, and other coaches noticed changes in her little gymnasts. Her influence was more pervasive than she thought, but inspiration has a way of seeping over, of spreading into places it is never intended to go. When light enters darkness, the light takes over. The coach said that people she didn't even know approached her and mentioned how much their student, granddaughter, or little sister loved her gymnastics class—that the gymnast still talks about the coach all the time. My favorite comment, though, was this one from the coach: "I did not realize that setting a good example and being an excellent role model can impact so many lives or a community in general."

It certainly can. A leader's inspiring influence can be extensive and people can be changed for the better because of it. Helping others see and adopt new values and do things on their own to make those values real in their lives, work, and character is the work of inspiring leadership.

Leaders who inspire do not merely rely on rational arguments or the fulfilling of material, temporal needs, or the training of new skills, like gymnastics. Those kinds of things we can count and hence control and manage. Leadership is what we do when we can't count it, control it, predict it, or measure it too well—things like loyalty, love, morale, esprit de corps, confidence, maturity, and so on. Leadership is the work of inspiring followers to adopt certain values and vision, and encouraging people, using principled-based sources of power, to act and control themselves accordingly. Leaders who inspire (and they all do) help others breathe in new ways of living.

Stories: The Essence of Vision

One way to be inspiring is to be inspired yourself. This is part of the personal preparation talked about earlier. Another way is to tell inspiring stories. There has been a recent groundswell in research supporting what most intuitive leaders already knew: stories matter—inspiring stories are even better. Sometimes called *leadership narratives*, stories are making a comeback. In fact, rather than investing a lot of time and effort (and resources) into creating vision statements, many are suggesting that we step back and create a few stories that illustrate our values in action. And as we have said, that is what a vision is: a picture in someone's mind and heart of what his or her values look like when they are acted out or put into practice. Leaders are good at telling vision stories.

One of the easiest stories to tell is *example*. Perhaps that is an odd thing to say, but a personal example is a story of how the values play out in our own day-to-day lives. As I work with individuals in any number of local, state, or federal agencies, I often hear that we should "lead by example" or that "leading by example is the most effective way." No argument with me at all—I agree. But the question is, why? Why is example so powerful a leadership tool or technique?

The answer is simple. Example is simply a very visual, real-life story. An example is a story that illustrates what the leaders think the values they keep talking about look like as they work to fulfill them in a way that does not betray them. In other words, leaders do what they say. They say what they do. They integrate what they feel is important with what they do. That is a powerful picture. As we know, followers as a whole are very good at eventually detecting when a "leader" is not walking the talk. Such unintegrated, two-faced "leaders" are very good at losing whatever followers they may have had. And without followers, there is no leader.

We said before that visions are pictures in our mind's eye of values in action. Examples are real-life pictures seen with real eyes, not with the mind's eye. That is the power of example, and it is in the same family as visions. Leadership by example is perhaps the best way to lead, because example may be the best kind of story told by the leader.

Example, though, is not the only story one can tell. We can simply tell *stories* or engage in the "art of the talk." It is fairly well acknowledged that this was one of Abraham Lincoln's consistent leadership techniques. He is well known for being a storyteller. More and more, historians and scholars are crediting Lincoln's storytelling as a critical element of his success as a leader. Lincoln persuaded, influenced, and inspired others through stories. His style of communication was a significant vehicle for promoting his vision. Not all of us may be as capable as Lincoln in our abilities to tell stories, but his lessons about that element of leadership are still highly relevant today.

Some stories may be based on the examples of others, and in that case we highlight the power of example again. Some stories have important imagery or illustrations of values played out in a life that can be applied to the lives of followers. Short stories seem to work the best. Perhaps that is because of time or attention span or the impact factor of "short and sweet." But stories seem to help followers choose to follow.

As an example, a story about Lincoln illustrates how telling tales can teach values that energize visions, giving a follower a chance to see how things should be done. The story goes that Lincoln found himself in a position to influence where certain roads would be built in the surrounding area. Local landowners believed such infrastructure could increase the value of their lands. One landowner came to Lincoln's office and, long story made short, offered Lincoln $5 if Lincoln would make sure a road went through his property. Lincoln just sat there with his feet on his desk. Another offer came and then another. Soon the landowner's bribe reached $50. At that point, Lincoln pulled back from his desk, took the man by the scruff of the neck, and threw him out of the office into the dusty street. The landowner was shocked and indignantly asked why Lincoln had done such a thing. Lincoln simply replied, "Because you were getting too close to my price." I don't know if the story is true. Much about Lincoln is legend and not always factual. But it does teach a principle or two about integrity, ethics, humility, self-awareness, self-discipline, and so on.

Like the story above, not all stories have a single interpretation, but it is in the interpretation that leaders have much of their influence. Leaders get to tell the moral of the story and that is an influential activity. I will never forget a story I heard growing up about a company that needed to hire a teamster in the Old West. It taught me about being responsible, careful, and honorable, and had various other impacts on my life as I kept reinterpreting it over time. A freight company needed to hire someone new to drive a team of horses and a wagon full of supplies over a rather treacherous mountain road. This would be a consistently traveled route, as settlers needed frequent supply runs, and the company saw this as a lucrative business opportunity. The first of three candidates came to the interview. The company representatives described the job and the route. Of note, they described one section of the route that required the driver to maneuver the wagon on a very narrow road on the edge of a cliff that angled steeply down the mountain. One false move and the wagon, cargo, horses, and driver would be gone.

When asked how he would handle such a dangerous terrain, the first candidate said he was such a good driver that he could control the wagon even if the cliff-side wheels were only six inches from the edge. The company representatives were impressed. Regarding the same problem, the second candidate boasted with relevant experiences that he could drive that wagon faster than anyone even if the cliff-side wheels were half a width off the edge of the cliff. Again, the representatives were impressed. The third candidate entered the room, and after being told of the hazardous mountain pass, looked at the panel members and said if he were to drive the wagon, he would steer the horses as far away from the edge of the cliff as possible, hugging the mountain wall, so as not to endanger the wagon, the cargo, or the horses ... and he would even slow down if needed. The third candidate was hired.

This story has multiple applications for sure, as many good stories do. It illustrates something about wisdom, safety, and respect for others' property. It also says something about responsibility, confidence that doesn't need boasting, and other valuable lessons. Explaining an application or an interpretation is part of the leadership activity. It is the leader's privilege to help others see the important values in the story and to see how those values look like in real-life scenarios.

In this way, there is no deception about the leader's intent and no manipulation of the follower. Instead, leaders' stories allow the followers to have a clear picture of what it would mean to follow. Such a clear picture ensures the choice to follow is a free-will choice, not manipulated or massaged by the slickness of a potential leader. It is that honest, volunteered commitment that is essential and will be explained more in chapter 5.

Some of the best stories ask followers to discern the values being expressed or the meaning of the story for themselves. The leader has the task of asking questions about the story and discussing applications to the current environment, purposes of work, and underlying values commitments. This conversation engages followers in the learning process, and in the values definition and vision creation process.

One such story is about a seashell store manager who expanded his business into the rock-selling business. It goes something like this. An owner and manager of a seashell store was experiencing great success. He decided to expand his business into selling beautiful rocks as well. He hired a helper and told him to go find rocks to sell. The helper went, found rocks, and brought them back. "These aren't the rocks I want. They won't sell. Go find me rocks." The helper did as he was told. He brought more rocks, different from the previous lot of rocks. The owner said again, "These aren't the rocks I am looking for. Go get me rocks." Once again, the helper did as he was instructed. Once again, the same frustrating response. Time and time again the help had the same experience doing work the boss didn't approve of. Finally, after one more order from the manager to go get him rocks, the helper turned around, walked out the shop door, and kept going.

Where did the helper go? To find more rocks and try again, to find a new job, to take some time for himself, to sulk and wait for someone to help him? Did he ever figure out what rocks his boss wanted? Did the *owner* even know? How did the helper deal with the frustration of working for a boss who never explained himself or his orders, or did he deal with it at all? Was the owner frustrated at how inept the helper was? Did he fire the helper? There are a lot of questions left when we reach the unsatisfactory conclusion. I find that this story has a few things to say regarding management and leadership and even life; and leader and follower have a chance to figure it out together. Indeed stories allow leader and follower to have a conversation about what is important. When the leader tells the story, he or she is placed in an influential position to express what is important or what ought to be important.

Another example of a story that is open to interpretation, but emphasizes certain values (like wisdom, humility, cleverness, and so on) over others, is about a hermit who lived in an old shack, miles from town and off the beaten track. He was quiet, kind, and unassuming, and though he stayed to himself much of the time, the townspeople grew to enjoy their interactions with him and eventually considered him the wisest person in those parts. Enter into the story a group of young people, led by a somewhat arrogant and prideful teenager. He was smart and popular for sure, and other teenage boys hung out with him—they followed him. But his approach to and outlook on life were less ennobling than they could have been. His pride was his driving value, and supremacy in competition with a dose of disdain for those of lesser standing was his vision. He had had enough of the story that the old hermit was wise.

This young man believed that he himself was wiser than the old hermit, and he would prove it. He gathered his followers (and perhaps a few curious onlookers who were still evaluating the efficacy of following him or not) and started walking down the path to the hermit's shack. Along the way, the young man stopped and caught a bird in his hand. He told the crowd his plan. "I will hold the bird in my cupped hands, out of sight, and then ask the old man whether this bird is alive or dead," the young man said. "If the old man says alive, I will crush it in my hands and show a dead bird, proving the old man isn't as smart as people say after all. If he says the bird is dead, I will open my hands and have the bird fly away. This plan will prove how much more clever I am. I will then be known as the wisest person in the region."

Finally, the crowd reached the shack. The young man asked the hermit whether the bird in his hand was alive or dead. The hermit stood in the doorway, not saying a word. The young man taunted him and after some time again asked the hermit, "Is the bird alive or dead?" The hermit finally said, with some concern in his voice, "It is as you wish it to be."

The young man was devastated. The crowd looked on, some in the crowd jeered at the young man, and some pleaded for him to give some wise reply, which never came. Eventually the crowd drifted away, leaving the young man to himself.

Stories are good at stressing some values over others. For example, there is a story (myth or reality, I am not sure) told to me years ago about an overnight package-delivery business that stressed the value of customer service. As the story goes, a loyal customer needed a package delivered overnight from New York to Boston. Unfortunately, the customer came to the store just minutes after closing. More importantly, he arrived just minutes after the delivery trucks had left. The customer pleaded with the store manager, who was sympathetic but who explained all the reasons why it couldn't be done. Nevertheless, the manager gave in and told the customer that he would take care of it. The package would be delivered overnight. The customer left contented; the manager stood there frantic. What to do? All normal channels for overnight delivery were unavailable.

Then the manager came upon an idea. He hailed a taxi. He told the driver the address in Boston where the package needed to be delivered and jumped in the cab with package in hand. Hours later, he had delivered the package, hopped back in the cab, and returned to the store in the wee hours of the morning, having traveled all night to fulfill his commitment to the customer. Perhaps the bravest thing he did was submit the taxi fare receipt (a substantial amount of money) to upper management with a letter explaining what had happened that night and asking for a reimbursement.

What did upper management do? What would you have done? It turns out that upper management honored the reimbursement request and even rewarded the manager for such creative devotion to customer service. When word got around to others in the company, the employees learned quickly that the organization was serious about customer service and appreciated the creativity and risk taking in honor of that value. (All the same, I bet they suggested not replicating this particularly creative and expensive solution very often.)

Another story that sticks with me about organizational values and how to approach the work being done deals with a public works director in a large metropolitan city. She tells the story that as a brand-new director of public works, she learned that a service orientation ought to be a part of any public servant's career—a lesson she incorporated into her leadership of the organization. Having grown up in the department, she was aware of almost all aspects of the department. She also knew the previous directors. During the first severe snowstorm of her tenure, she decided to go out on the snowplows herself. She thought it would be a good example to the others. She found herself plowing the streets in the neighborhood of a retired department director. As she pulled around the corner, she saw the former director. In his advanced age, he was out there in an old public works jacket with a shovel in hand, shoveling out snow from around cars and on the sidewalks where city snowplows couldn't reach. She marveled at the sight. She began to think to herself that when there was a need to serve the public, this public servant was there. She made an inventory of her life and wondered if she had that same service orientation. She took from the experience two things: the importance of a public service orientation, and that to serve quietly and consistently wherever it was needed is a hallmark of the true public servant. She had refined for herself the value of public service, and she used the story as a way of explaining such public service to her employees.

What stories really do (if told with leadership intent in mind) is reveal the personal, the emotional, and the rational—that is, the values, principles, perspectives, and practices important to the leader. The hope is that such things will also be important to the follower. Stories are a part of the leadership responsibility of vision. Stories remind the leader what is important because the leader picks what story to tell and then tells it the leader's way. These stories also serve to inspire the followers to choose, to do, and to be what is necessary in the cooperative work that is to be done.

Points to Ponder

1. How does the idea of painting a mental picture help you understand the nature and power of vision?
2. How is example a type of vision?
3. If a vision statement is necessary, what should it be like? What should it do?
4. How does knowing yourself and others help you prepare and present visions? What role does reflection have in helping you know yourself?
5. What are some tools we can use to "figure people out" so that we can shape stories and visions in ways they can receive them?
6. What does it mean to have a vision that is leader-centric but follower focused?
7. How does inspiration play a role in the notion of vision? How does inspiration differ from motivation, if at all?

8. How have others inspired you as you observe their example or hear their vision stories?
9. Why is storytelling a useful skill in explaining visions? Do you think you can be a skilled storyteller as you practice the craft of visioning?
10. What are some of your favorite stories, and what values do they reveal?

Quotables

1. "Leadership is the capacity to translate vision into reality." —Warren G. Bennis, author
2. "Vision is the art of seeing the invisible." —Jonathan Swift
3. "Where there is no vision the people perish." —Proverbs 29:18
4. "In the long run men hit only what they aim at." —Henry David Thoreau
5. "If you want to build a ship, don't drum up people to collect wood and don't assign them tasks and work, but rather teach them to long for the endless immensity of the sea." —Antoine de Saint-Exupéry, aviator and writer

Practical Activities

1. *Figuring People Out.* To practice figuring out what matters to others, take time to walk around and observe your current workplace or somewhere else you spend a lot of time. As you do this, use the tools outlined in the chapter to create a "People Report" that outlines artifacts and their possible meanings, common and uncommon stories and their application to the workplace, relationships and how people interact with others, and the rituals and what they are meant to reinforce in the workplace. Review this report, talk it over with others you trust, and practice being observant in other situations as well. You can also review the report to see whether there are any areas you can influence in the workplace that might change the vision or culture of the place.
2. *Storytelling.* Storytellers tell stories. So they have to have stories to tell. Take time to memorize or create stories that you can use on the spur of the moment. Practice telling them. Put your own style into them and make them your own. You can start by learning stories others have written that tell a point you would like to make. Eventually, create your own stories from your personal experiences. Keep them short. Practice telling them again and again. A goal may be to have a booklet of stories that you can tell from time to time. Adding to that booklet will have its own benefits as you find stories that really explain values in the way you want them to.

Notes

1. Rivka Grundstein-Amado, "Bilateral Transformational Leadership: An Approach for Fostering Ethical Conduct in Public Service Organizations," *Administration & Society* 31 (1999): 250.

2. See Martha F. Miser, "Vision: The Engine of Change," Aduro Consulting LLC, 2006, 1, http://www.aduroconsulting.net/resources/The-Power-of-Vision_Aduro.pdf; see also Robert Ajemian, "Where Is the Real George Bush?" *Time*, January, 26, 1987, where the statement was first reported.

3. Peter Salovey and John D. Mayer, "Emotional Intelligence," *Imagination, Cognition, and Personality* 9 (1990): 185–211.

4. Richard L. Hughes, Robert C. Ginnett, and Gordon J. Curphy, *Leadership: Enhancing the Lessons of Experience* (Boston: McGraw-Hill, 1993), 189.

5. Ibid., 195.

6. For example see Jack Mezirow (ed.), *Learning as Transformation: Critical Perspectives on a Theory in Process* (San Francisco: Jossey-Bass, 2000), and Judy O'Neil and Victoria J. Marsick, *Understanding Action Learning: Theory into Practice* (New York: Amacom, 2007).

7. Peter Senge, *The Fifth Discipline: The Art and Practice of the Learning Organization* (New York: Doubleday, 1990), 223.

8. Hughes, Ginnett, and Curphy, *Leadership*, 241.

9. Ibid.

Chapter 4

Vectors: Pathways of Practice

Just as visions operationalize for followers what the leader's values look like in real life, vectors help followers see the path to fulfilling the vision. It is to *vectors* we now turn. First, we need to determine why we use the term itself, beyond the consistency of using words that begin with the letter *V*. The term *vector* has as one of its meanings (and the one we are concerned with here) the direction and magnitude of something. More precisely for our purposes, vectors deal with the "what," the "where to," the "how," and the "how much" of what we are to do in order to fulfill the vision. The word comes from the Latin and had the original meaning "to carry" or "to convey." In this sense, vector as a leadership element is to carry the vision forward in terms of outlining actual things to do or to convey to the followers what it is that is required or what they must do to make the vision a reality.

It is the work of leadership to outline the vectors to be done, the steps to be taken, or the path to follow, to make sure our vision is realized and our values fulfilled. Noted leadership writer Stephen Covey, in his book *The 8th Habit*, suggests that there is a need for discipline in carrying out a vision. Such discipline means paying the price to make a vision a reality—"dealing with the hard, pragmatic, brutal facts of reality and doing what it takes to make things happen."[1] Such is the leadership notion of *vectors*. It is getting things done, but done in a certain way consistent with values and vision to help others develop (or discipline) themselves into people better able to get things done.

There are many ways to fulfill a particular vision, so the leader's job must be, at least partly, to outline clearly what he or she thinks the steps ought to be. It is a creative process on the part of the leader, and the steps are almost necessarily aligned with the values of the leader. Vectors that are outlined for followers give them another opportunity to exercise their willingness to follow. For instance, I could be a follower who chooses to accept the values and the vision, but perhaps I don't feel comfortable with the vectors, the steps to be taken to accomplish the vision. In that sense, I may not be as strong or committed a follower as I could be. If I find myself agreeing fully with the values, the vision, *and* the vectors, then my inspiration, enthusiasm, commitment, and loyalty are that much more enhanced.

These vectors might be more commonly called "objectives," "key result areas," "critical success factors," "long-term goals," or "strategic goals." These kinds of terms are found in literature on mission and strategic planning, and the notion of vector fits squarely in this camp. In fact, if I were to have four or five vectors (statements of what we will do and how we know when we did it) and then put them together into a sentence with semicolons in between, I would end up with a pretty solid mission statement for the group or organization I am trying to lead. That mission statement would therefore by linked directly to the vision (because it is the way we are to fulfill it) and therefore relate directly to the values that make us who we are.

It is that linkage that is partially the beauty and the purpose of leadership. People like to know where they stand and how their work fits together with the overall organization. Knowing these things helps them have a place in the world and be assured that what they are doing is worthwhile and useful. Vectors play a key role in making sure these connections happen.

A Word on "*Misions*"

There has been much written on and a lot of consulting about visions and missions, vision statements and mission statements. Some experts say missions come first and then visions. Others say visions must come before missions. Some don't link the two at all but simply advocate for both. They say vision and mission statements are for different purposes and hence are relatively distinct in their development and application. Some say missions need to have a quantitative nature to them (their de facto direction). Some say visions are to be future oriented and have implicit or explicit timelines attached. Some say both need quantitative orientations and timelines; some say neither is necessary. So much written, so much money spent on retreats and experts. Very little agreement and perhaps less sense come from all of these discussions and approaches. Don't get me wrong. The elements of vision and mission are important, but I myself have seen mission statements that look a lot like vision statements and vice versa.

I have played with the notion that we should create a new term combining vision and mission into one idea: the *mision* (pronounced "mizhon," a mixture of vision and mission). This notion would try to combine the many ideas on vision and mission into a simple notion: we need to know what we are to do and perhaps even why, how much of it, and when we know we did it. Sometimes the terms themselves simply get in the way of the basic ideas trying to be expressed.

Obviously, I ultimately did not move forward with *misions*. I opted instead to try to define the basic notion by explaining two terms: *vision* and *vector*. In this way, you may see that vision implies a preeminent role with respect to vectors. Vision becomes a prerequisite for vectors; vectors are intimately and necessarily linked to vision because they operationalize the vision in people's lives. But while vision precedes vector, without vectors, visions have very little chance of coming to fruition. Vectors ensure a vision is not simply a dream.

Operationalizing Vision: The Pathways to Practice

This practical side of vector is appealing to many. Those who have a penchant for getting things done often skip all of that values and vision stuff and go right to the vectors. Although the go-getter attitude is admirable, the leaping-before-we-look approach may be more dangerous to a group or organization than a looking-before-we-leap method. Saying that, though, I recognize the asking-forgiveness-rather-than-permission tactic is often a useful one in the world of leadership and organizational dynamics. So nothing but respect can be given to people who can get things done well, especially if they also know why those things are important to get done and just how it is we develop the criteria to determine what done "well" actually is.

What does it mean, then, to operationalize a vision or to help make the vision a reality in the lives of leader and follower? It involves aligning the following issues to the vision: what to do, where it will take us, how much of it we do, how we know we did enough, and how we know we did it well.

In general, these issues take into account what we commonly do in step-by-step planning, or goal setting, or performance measurement and metrics, or organizational alignment between goals and actions. We often forget that followers need and want to do these kinds of things, to be involved, or at least to believe the results of such activities completed by others are valid. The question of validity more often than not is a question of whether the vectors and the plans attached to them are congruent with the followers' perception of the values and vision the leader expresses.

Although the goals and subgoals, objectives and subobjectives, and the plans attached to them all are essential, we will touch only briefly on them.

In chapter 6, we will discuss further how the Four Vs help in strategic thinking and planning initiatives. But for now, the focus on vectors is a high-level focus—the proverbial 50,000-foot level. Vectors are designed to give the general areas of concern for the work to be done. They categorize the work in some ways. As John Mercer, former mayor of Sunnyvale, California, suggested, high-level strategic goals need to be measurable but need not be quantifiable. An example of a measurable but not quantifiable, overarching goal was the goal to reach the moon by the end of the 1960s. We could know if it were achieved, but there weren't any real quantifiable elements (or things that are counted and accounted for routinely) that are by themselves evidence of success.

That example teaches us that for vectors to be measurable they are to be "knowable when achieved." We have to know that it is being done and ultimately that it is done. There ought to be a way to make sure the leader and followers know they are on the right track and the vision is becoming reality. Vectors allow that to happen.

The only caveat is that some vectors do not end. For instance, one nonprofit I worked with developed a vector they called "organizational sustainability"—the capacity for the organization to continue to exist as the organization it was designed to be. For a nonprofit, this is often a formidable task. But it is also a task that will not be completed. By definition, it is an ongoing vector for the life of the organization. We can measure its achievement over time in both qualitative and quantitative ways, but it is an achievement in progress, not an achievement in completion.

Therefore vector is the summary of work, or categories of work, that is to be done to fulfill the organization's purpose. It is a summary of work that also has within it the direction our work takes us while at the same time delimiting the scope of the work in terms of magnitude, metrics, and meaning.

For example, a small midwestern town developed vectors after considering the shared values of its people and developing a vision story about the city. The vectors included:

1. Promote the marketing of the city, highlighting its schools, businesses, churches, and recreational areas in brochures and websites.
2. Build a new community center.
3. Establish one economic development agency to recruit businesses and to market the industrial park.
4. Work with the local council of governments to update the city's Comprehensive Plan of Development.
5. Build strong new leadership and more citizen engagement in public affairs.

These might seem too specific to some, but they were fitting for the purposes at hand for the community. They offered a direction for city leaders to exert their efforts and specified certain deliverables to help them achieve their overall values and vision.

A larger western city developed these phrases as summary vector areas that guided its current and future activities: Guided Growth, Quality of Life, Public Safety, Economy Strength, Maintained and Developed City Infrastructure, Constructed City Image. These are more generic in nature than the previous list but serve similar functions. They direct action in fulfillment of vision and values.

Workers at a nonprofit organization in Minnesota that deals with delivering direct social services developed vectors they felt would help them overcome the hard times they had recently encountered due to natural disasters that devastated their facilities and hence their finances. They summarized them into phrases that depicted the areas of focus and began to organize themselves in terms of these vector areas: Cost Awareness, Open Arms, Quality Atmosphere, Holistic Impacts, Solid Service Reputation, Sustainability. Another much larger social service organization in Chicago had developed these vectors in a time of growth:

- Work with families, organizations, and public systems to build healthy and safe communities.
- Advocate for policies and services that help individuals reclaim control of their lives.
- Provide services to help individuals overcome addictive and other behavioral illnesses and their consequences.
- Respect the dignity, value, and potential of all people.

It is easy to see how these examples of vectors have a connection to values and a vision for the organization. They help differentiate their organizations from other organizations while at the same time grounding their work in a values and vision context.

The Link between Thinking and Doing[2]

The bottom line is that visions are merely dreams, as they say, if they are not or cannot be accomplished. Vectors turn dreams into achievable visions. Vectors provide the way, the direction, and magnitude of work required to make the vision realized in the lives of the leader and followers. All too often, though, visions and vectors (or *missions*, as they may more commonly be called) are not linked. Even more often, we find that strategic plans based on organizational missions are not linked to a clear organizational vision, let alone visions linked to values.

Much of this is because strategic planning efforts do not require such linkages to values and vision and yet may still remain a potent organizational and management tool. In fact, there is a growing literature on the difference between or the relationship of strategic thinking and strategic planning, the former being argued to be more focused on leadership ideas and the latter on management.

Linking the two is a side benefit of the Four Vs and is a major benefit to followers who seek to link the heart and soul of the group or organization with the nitty-gritty things that are done day to day: the thinking and the doing, the feeling and the planning. It is part of the work of leadership to make these linkages for their followers. Understanding the links allows the followers a clearer picture of what it is they chose to follow (which enhances the freedom they used to make that choice), and it allows the followers to understand that what they do and how they do it matter or fit into the work being done in the organization.

Looking at two typical extremes of the strategic planning/thinking continuum, we can first see how not making linkages is both common and incomplete. This approach may be called the How Approach. The How Approach refers to plans being made to determine only how something is to be done, with little thought about the something itself. In other words, this approach takes as a given the work to be done and then goes about trying to get it all done well. The How Approach implies the existence of a predetermined set of objectives and/or a mechanism to achieve them. This is most apparent in public sector agencies where missions and mandates and even timelines are often handed down by legislative bodies to public mangers. Management, then, conducts strategic planning to determine the most appropriate means (set of actions) to achieve those objectives.

Mission objectives and goals are assumed from the nature of the business and made explicit by management so that plans can be made to methodically account for activity designed to achieve the end result.[3] However, no attempt at examining the assumptions that predetermine the mission and the objectives is undertaken. The process is a technical one akin to merely filling out forms, without questioning the forms.

At the other end of the continuum is the Why-What-How Approach. In this approach, there is an obvious strategic logic, but perhaps a logic that is more holistic in nature. Strategic thinking is understanding that the world

FIGURE 4.1. Continuum of Strategic Thinking and/or Planning Approaches

Comfort with Control   *Comfort with Uncertainty*

How	**What-How**	**What-Why-How**	**Why-What-How**
Strategy as Plan	Strategy as Business Position	Mission-Based Strategy	Strategic Thinking or Vision-Based Strategy

may not always work in linear, methodical ways—that organizations and those working within them must become agile, flexible, relationship-savvy, and wise as they continually adapt plans to meet emergent and even ambiguous situations.[4]

Such skills require leaders to be clear about themselves and their values or biases and those of the organizations that sprout from them the leader's values and biases. Personal and organizational introspection are an essential part. In other words, we begin to understand the power of assumption and challenge it. For example, we begin to question the forms we fill out to see whether they ask what we want, look right, or even need to exist at all. It is a systems approach recognizing the benefits of a holistic view of organizations, allowing us to challenge the ideas of control and stability while embracing the internal and external context of the organization and the organizational work.[5]

Two other approaches are noted in Figure 4.1. The What-How Approach suggests that we first establish what we are in business for and then determine if certain *hows* are even appropriate and how other *hows* are to be accomplished to fit into the established purpose (the what) of the organization. The What-Why-How Approach adds an element of ambiguity to the mix as it creates scenarios and options to fulfill different *whats* with different *hows*. This is a creative and contingency-based planning approach that begins to free us from tradition and allow the system to flex with different organizational or environmental variables.

As we become more sophisticated in our thinking about organizations, we basically need to comprehend why things operate the way they do. We need to understand that organizational wisdom comes not from programming and prediction, but rather from an understanding of human motivations, formal and informal organizational values, culture, and inter- and intraorganizational relationships. With a firmer grasp of the *whys* of social and organizational interaction, we then can have a clearer picture of what we should, could, can, and cannot do, within those contexts.[6] In fact, it is a process of defining the values and culture, organizational paradigms, and purposes of an organization (sometimes an effort fraught with discomfort).

However, as we tackle that discomfort, the *whats* (or vectors) that emerge become much more meaningful in terms of shaping individual and organizational behavior because they are based on individual and organizational values. From there, the *hows* are more informed, more realistic, taking into account the qualitative as well as the quantitative aspects of action planning. The Why-What-How Approach requires a focus on relationships, leverage points, and outcome measures of success rather than concrete milestones, step-by-step procedures, or statistical reports.[7]

Such an approach provides meaning to the followers. Such an approach links the *whys* with the *whats* with the *hows* so that followers know where they stand and why. And they know what to do and why. This honors their individuality, capacities, and frankly their innate right to choose for themselves. Such a context can create powerfully committed and loyal followers.

Thinking, Not Planning

For this reason, no matter how important focusing on goals, outcomes, and processes are, strategic thinking must be founded on more basic principles if it is to be distinct from planning. When people in organizations are clear about their real (not apparent) values commitments, their purpose and meaning, they can then begin to see why their personal goals and outcomes are either sensible or incongruent with the group goals. They also begin to see whether their actions are reasonable, time-bound, or too inflexible.[8]

Starting with goals does not allow us to determine whether the goals are valid or proper, nor if the subsequent actions planned to achieve those goals will work as dictated. Values and purpose become the measuring rod and the criteria to determine the efficacy of any goals, outcomes, formal or informal processes, or activities. The organizational skin and bones that are goals and outcomes become enlivened by and infused with organizational spirit, which are the values, vision, and underlying reasons for being.[9] Strategic planning works on the skin and bones; strategic thinking works on organizational soul.[10]

Four ideas can help us remember to make linkages for our followers to allow them to follow with wisdom, clarity, and commitment. First, and this goes without saying, *adopt a values, vision, and vector orientation rather than a goals, objectives, and tactics mentality*. Leadership is the prework to strategic planning, which ultimately leads to specific managerial tasks.

In sum, the reliance on and prioritization of values are the main things that drive strategic thinking, whereas the achievement of goals and the control of actionable events drive strategic planning.[11]

Second, *see yourself as an organizational philosopher more than as a technical expert.* Organizational philosophers devote much effort in untangling the complexities of life within organizations. Organizational philosophers love to learn about their organizations, the grander contexts in which they operate, and the interactions within the organization structure, be it formal or informal. They foster continual organizational learning—the stuff of organizational wisdom. They want to know how it all works and see the patterns.[12] They want to influence the collective toward the wisest use of resources and the wisest relationships among the people.[13] Strategic thinkers (or organizational philosophers) ask important questions and integrate the answers. What is the purpose of the organization? Why does it exist? Where did it come from? Why is it here? What might make it go away, and what happens to the people and to the original reason for being if the organization does cease to exist? What makes life in the organization meaningful? How does the organization fit into the grand scheme of other organizations? Is the formal structure of the organization indicative of the realities of organizational involvement or do the informal structures and networks better define the organization's character, values, and culture? These and other essential questions are what real strategic thinking consists of, because they give us a clearer vision of the *whys* of organizational life so that the *whats* and *hows* make more sense and are more efficacious.[14]

For example, people in a particular local government construction permitting office saw themselves traditionally as engineers, inspectors, and "paper-pushers." Their mission was clear and routine. When asked to become a part of the economic development activities, reach out to customers, and start a building-ambassador program, they saw no sense in it. The tasks they were now asked to perform were not only foreign to them, but they were also contrary to what they had been doing for years. The tasks were developed by planners (with no involvement by the frontline implementers) who got the new mission from above and started making it happen. But the skill sets and sense of purpose the permitting group had developed over time did not match up to the new direction of the organization. Frustration, confusion, and setbacks became the norm. Only when efforts were made to explain the new direction and offer the *whys* of the new programs did any progress begin to be seen. But even then, the workers were never truly committed and they often changed the tasks to fit their own, time-tested, purposes.

Strategic thinkers would understand that changing tasks alone is insufficient to achieving a real programmatic shift. They would see the big picture and help people repaint it so that the new tasks fit and the new purpose made sense. Creating steps and milestones is not always enough; people need sense making and meaning as well.

Third, *concentrate on the flow of information and the quality of relationships that emerge, rather than the control of information.* By letting go of the control-and-prediction mentality of strategic planning and programming, organizations by necessity assume different foundations to organizational activity. Leadership in this sense is about maintaining organizations as identifiable entities over time, while changing and adapting to meet future demands. Rather than restrict and control information coming from within and without an organization (as strategic planners like to do), leaders must recognize the importance of free and easy access to information.[15] This further links the followers to the activities of the group or organization. It also allows them to be active participants in the work of the group. And since they chose to work together, such free flow of information serves only to solidify that choice time and time again.

Fourth, *learn to accept and work with ambiguity and the qualitative nature of organizations, rather than try to control and quantify all organizational endeavors.* Trying to control what may be inherently uncontrollable (people involved in processes and organizations) is an organizational stance devoid of maturity and wisdom. A comfort with ambiguity emerges as leaders learn to ask the right questions and accept their limited perspective while seeking to gain a higher one.[16]

Being able to shape vectors that make vision achievable is a critical activity of leadership. It brings people together with the work they do, but it also brings people together with the organizational overlay in which they operate. People feel more comfortable with their decision to follow, and they become more active, interesting, and valuable followers. They see the values and vision as real and useful. They also see them as driving the work and linking their contributions to the overall whole. Such is the purpose and power of vectors.

Points to Ponder

1. What is the essence or purpose of vectors?
2. What does the term *mision* help us remember about popular literature on missions and visions?

3. How does linking vision to practical daily activities help us engage potential followers?
4. How do vectors help us align the strategic with the tactical?
5. Explain what a good measurement can do for the work of an organization as it implements vectors and goals and objectives.
6. How do vectors help us distinguish ourselves from other organizations?
7. What are some key elements of strategic thinking and strategic planning?
8. Reexamine the four ideas outlined in the chapter to help us remember to make linkages for our followers? Why are they useful? How can you incorporate them into the work you do?

Quotables

1. "Go as far as you can see; when you get there, you'll be able to see farther." — J. P. Morgan, industrialist
2. "It is very dangerous to go into eternity with possibilities which one has one-self prevented from becoming realities. A possibility is a hint from God. One must follow it." —Sören Kierkegaard, Danish philosopher
3. "Vision is not enough. It must be combined with venture. It is not enough to stare up the steps, we must step up the stairs." —Vaclav Havel, last president of Czechoslovakia

Practical Activities

1. *Seeing Vectors around You.* Most organizations engage in vectors, though not every organization has outlined them explicitly. As you volunteer in community or church or interest-based groups, try to discern the vectors that the group is trying to achieve. Are they evident? If not, how can you figure out what they are? Did those vectors play a role in your choice to join the group? How and why? As you practice discerning the vectors of groups you belong to, you will be better able to develop vectors for other organizations.
2. *Strategic Thinking and Planning.* Consider an organization you currently work in or associate with. Try mapping out the values, vision, vectors, and strategic goals and objectives. Place them in a cascading picture or other organized manner. If there are holes or areas that are difficult to discern, be creative in filling those holes in with what you think should be done. As you analyze current organizations, you will gain skills in developing organizations on your own or shaping them in ways you lead.

Notes

1. Stephen R. Covey, *The 8th Habit: From Effectiveness to Greatness* (New York: Free Press, 2004), 65.

2. Some of the material in this section has been published previously in Matthew R. Fairholm, "Leadership and Organizational Strategy," *The Innovation Journal: The Public Sector Innovation Journal*, 14, no. 1 (2009): article 3. Used by permission.

3. Ibid., 4.
4. Ibid., 5.
5. Ibid.
6. Ibid., 6.
7. Ibid.
8. Ibid., 8.
9. Ibid.
10. Ibid.
11. Ibid., 9.
12. Ibid.
13. Ibid.
14. Ibid.
15. Ibid., 11–12.
16. Ibid., 12–13.

Chapter 5

Voice: People of Practice

The topic of *voice* in the leadership relationship is to me the most vital. It deserves attention because it is not commonly discussed (at least not explicitly) in leadership books. To be basic, *voice* is the V-word for choice. It has to do with volition, freedom, or individual agency to act for oneself. Voice reminds us that where there is no choice in the relationship among people, there can be no leadership. At best, perhaps there is management; at worst, there is oppression or tyranny or manipulation or authoritarianism. But there is no leadership without the protection of and the opportunity to have people choose to lead, but more importantly choose to follow.

Voice reminds us that leadership is a volunteer activity. We choose to lead at times and we choose to follow a lot in life. For example, how often have you chosen your boss? It happens, but it is not common. Usually, as you formally join a group, you are told that so-and-so is your supervisor/manager/boss, and during orientation you most likely have a chance to meet her. Maybe you met this person in an interview process and you decided she was an acceptable boss before you took the job, so in that sense you made a choice. But generally speaking you are given your boss without much choice in the matter.

But although we usually do not choose our boss, we always, always choose who we follow. We always choose our leaders. And what is that choice based on? It is based on the values, the vision, and the vectors that the leader has outlined and with which we feel agreement or affinity or to which we have a desire to become united.

A Matter of Individual Choice

Voice reminds us that it is all a matter of individual choice. Recall what was said in earlier chapters: understanding leadership has more to do with understanding the followers than it does understanding someone who holds a position of power. This is because whether or not someone is ulti-mately a leader depends entirely on whether or not another person chooses to follow him or her.

In leadership, it is all about volunteerism. In other words, leaders recog-nize that followers are, of their own volition, choosing to engage with the values, vision, and vectors outlined by the leader. An international aid vol-unteer I know (we'll call her Mary) serving in the Ukraine shortly after the fall of the Berlin Wall learned just how real voice is in an organization. She learned that how voice is exercised matters for the whole organization. Mary served with other volunteers assigned to teach English in a variety of settings. Quickly, she deduced that there were at least three ways to exer-cise voice: *reject* the values, vision, and vectors; *disregard* the values, vision, and vectors; or *accept* the values, vision, and vectors.

Rejection took the face of a volunteer who decided that what Ukrainians needed more than English skills were waterbeds. Mary told of how he flaunted his American status, and instead of being the kind of volunteer envi-sioned by the program, he seemed to be promoting a waterbed import/export business. This was no easy thing for others in the organization. Mary observed that the Americans in town were widely gossiped about and watched with fascination. She and her Ukrainian colleagues and students had gotten word of his activities and were saddened and a bit offended. Furthermore, she was repeatedly asked if the international organization she belonged to was really a serious and respectable organization. Indeed, when workers reject the cause behind the work, when they reject the values, vision, and vectors, the impact on others is not isolated. Others in the organization feel the consequences of the rejection too. Some are emboldened by a mem-ber's rejection to stay even more firm to the cause, but certainly some are persuaded over time to reject the values as well.

Mary described a second volunteer who seemed to simply *disregard* or ignore the values, vision, and vectors of the international organization's purpose and instead fell back on her own interests and perceived needs. This volunteer put in her time for the most part, but she had other prior-ities, other personal needs, that the organization apparently wasn't fulfill-ing. She spent much of her time fulfilling those needs rather than pursuing the organization's cause. There is perhaps a more subtle conse-quence within the organization in this scenario, but there is an impact. Sure, work is being done, but enthusiasm, inspiration, and commitment are absent in the worker, and performance ultimately suffers. Virus-like, that kind of blasé work ethic spreads and makes the organization look and feel bad. Mary commented that other volunteers began to hear negative feedback from Ukrainians about this unprofessional behavior. Mary and her colleagues were annoyed, she said, that they had to do damage control, trying repeatedly to convince others that the international aid workers were indeed capable and trustworthy.

A third volunteer who *accepted* and seemed most committed to the values, vision, and vectors (like the vast majority of those involved in the program) created new projects, taught new seminars, received positive feedback, developed trust within the larger community, and otherwise felt content that her goals, congruent with the goals of the organization, had been fulfilled. Although this one volunteer admitted to not perfectly living up to all she could have in terms of the goals, rules, and procedures, her heart was true to the principles and cause—and that made all the difference. The impact here may be obvious. Enthusiasm pervaded the work. Relationships of trust provided opportunity for personal growth among the volunteers and those served. The work was being done as with the second volunteer, but this time it was being done in a way that both reinforced and fulfilled the values and vision intended by the enterprise.

These stories of volunteers are used only to highlight the options of voice—rejecting leadership, disregarding leadership, and willingly accepting leadership—and remind us that we are all volunteers, or choosers, of one type or another. These types of reactions to leadership can take place in any organization. However, true followers are true volunteers on the journey, volunteers in the collective activity undertaken by the group. They don't reject, they don't dismiss, but rather they choose to accept and adopt the leadership at hand.

Imagine an Organization of Volunteers

To be clear, management does not require volunteers. Management requires subordinates willing to accept and perform directives based on the authority and position of the one giving the directives. Although there is a choice to obey the directive and adhere to the management's rules, there is no requirement that people be committed to the cause, the boss, or the organization. They do what they are told (requiring some modicum of choice, which is probably exercised when the first decision to join the group occurred) in exchange for some reward that the subordinate values. But that is all management needs. Leadership, however, is all about individuals choosing (and frequently rechoosing) to follow a leader who exercises influence, persuasion, and strength of character, but who does not rely on positional authority or crass uses of power.

Imagine if everyone in the organization acted as if everyone else were a volunteer in the work of the organization and that they were not required to be at work by some contract or implicit transactional agreement. Workers come to work because they feel the work meaningful and they receive internal rewards (even inspiration) from what they contribute to others. Those in positions of hierarchy could not be guaranteed that workers would return to work the next day unless the workers decided it was still worthwhile to do so. And so those positional figures would need to inspire, set examples, reiterate and remind others of the values, vision, and vectors at play. They would need to be inspiring and influential, not organizational politicians and tacticians. They would have to assume that all workers were volunteers engaged in the work because they believe in the work, not because they received transactional benefits of value (like a paycheck). They would act so that the workers continue to want to come to work every day. When we assume people are volunteers capable of acting for themselves and making choices, then we resist acting upon them so that they achieve "my goals" irrespective of "their goals." It would be an organization where people walked the talk and lived up to shared values. It would be a very different organization than many people are used to.

Furthermore, it would be an organization where everyone worked to earn other people's trust and cooperation over time. This type of organization would feel comfortable to a salesman in a technology company I learned of. He described his boss by saying there was nothing fake about him; that he was real, never seeming to be parroting some book detailing "how to be a good manager" but rather just being a good person. This salesman said that if employees were in a rut, the boss would sit down with them and talk about not just work but their whole life. If something was wrong at home, he noticed, and he spent a lot of time counseling. If there was a gripe about the company, the upper management and their practices, he would side with the employee first and listen as if the employee was "preaching to the choir." If the boss ever used any authority, it was the authority earned in managing a team that gave him clout with the upper management. The salesman also noted that the boss had a life as well, and he let the group in on his personal ideas and interests. People came to work because the boss was there, and the boss made people want to come to work and colabor with him. The boss was doing leadership. When the volunteer aspect of leadership is remembered, workers are no longer seen explicitly or implicitly as "cogs in the industrial machine." They are seen as people able to make choices and cooperate in the collective activity.

A Reminder about Individual Choice

We see, then, that a capacity for doing leadership must be the ability to both understand and encourage the way people make choices, especially choices to engage with others in some collaborative, collective activity. In practice, we all know that individual people make up groups, but often the unit of analysis in leadership focuses so much on the group that we lose sight of the individual.

This should not be taken too far, of course, as a lot of books and articles on leadership certainly focus almost entirely on the individual. Researchers look at the individual in terms of people at the top of the organization chart and what he or she can be like or do to change, progress, or improve the group they oversee. Or they focus on more general notions of the individual and his or her personal preparation, character, values, agency, and so forth, no matter where the individual in the hierarchy.

However, very often leadership is thought of as a group activity, not an individual activity. Useful as it is to see the unit of analysis as groups or teams, more useful it is to see that individuals should remain the fundamental unit of analysis in leadership. It is the individual with his or her capacities and rights that form the families, the groups, the institutions, and the societies we hope to lead. It is the idea of free choice that individuals have and the very choices they make that form the foundation of any leadership relationship.

To determine what leadership is and then to encourage people to engage in it requires that we figure out how it is that people choose, how people help others to choose or to act for themselves, and how to distinguish that individual choice from the activities of people who impose or act upon others. Central to leadership studies is the study of choice, moral agency, volition, and even volunteerism.

The Impact of Choice

Something happens when individuals choose to engage in a common purpose or activity. When enthusiasm, meaning, and purpose are evident, individuals begin to come together. They define, and refine, the work being done, and a cooperative relationship emerges. In a real sense, the individuals change too. They grow in their capacities, and they have to refine themselves and their interactions to encourage the relationships to continue. Understanding emerges in the work, but also in the characters of the people involved. Excellent work is often the result, as are more excellent people. Individuals are better than they used to be acting alone, but they do not stop being individuals. They simply become changed individuals, better people for having the chance to interact with others and produce high-quality results and meaningful relationships. And the groups are better than they used to be too because they are made up of better, more united individuals.

This change in people mainly occurs in three ways. First, values and aspirations and purpose become more efficacious, more real, and more meaningful as individuals share and come together around those values, aspirations, and purposes. They also become refined and honed as they make public declarations (through either actions or words) about what they believe is important and useful and meaningful. They become, in a sense, more moral, or at least they become more confident in the morality grounding their collaborative efforts.

Second, they become more adept at the work being done. Seeing the capacities and qualities of others, they begin to learn new and better and perhaps just different ways to get things done. They become more humble about their positions and capacities and more appreciative of other people's positions and capacities. They become more competent and better able to wisely choose future work, work processes, and work partners.

Third, they become more savvy as actors within society. They begin to better understand what does not work and what does not add meaning or morality to collective action as much as what does. They are better able to see the positions of others, their power sources, and their sources of meaning and purpose. They are better able to choose wisely between alternatives because of it. They begin to see that when position and rank and title and hierarchy are not present (or are unimportant to the leadership phenomenon), then they need to focus more on cooperation, relationships of shared power, and synergistic innovation.

Indeed, leadership as differentiated from management, headship, or the like is a phenomenon of relationship, individual choice, and personal growth. With these individual results, the society made up of such individuals reaps the associated benefits. We cannot, in the discussions of leadership, allow the individual to be lost in the process of bringing individuals together. There are some practical and normative reasons for that.

Individual Choice: The Practical

The practical reason is that for leadership to work, multiple individuals with a variety of values foundations, policy biases, program customs, and missions and visions need to develop relationships based on a shared power model, cohesive mutual values, and cooperative structures. That is a mouthful. Fundamentally, it is about individuals choosing to be in colabor with other individuals. And it is the choosing that sets leadership apart from other collective action like, for instance, management, oppression, manipulation, coercion, and the like. In fact, the act of choosing is the single most important element of the leadership relationship; and free choice is an individual act.

To encourage the acting of individuals to make the choice to work together with others, rather than developing ways to act upon others with or without their complete consent, is *the* act of leadership. Remember in previous chapters we learned that leaders are those who have followers, and we have to learn how to get people to choose to follow us rather than other people. Understanding the individual and the individual act of choosing is central to leadership discussions and action. Without a real focus on the individual and individual choice in the activities of leadership, the activities will lose much of their worth and usefulness.

As we break down certain elements of choice, we reveal fundamental principles and preeminent concerns of leadership. Individual choice requires four conditions: opposition, rules and sanctions, recognition of moral rights and moral wrongs (good choices and bad choices), and a protected and enduring freedom to choose. Leadership requires us to focus on and reinforce these conditions.

Opposition

It might sound simplistic, though perhaps not obvious, but leadership depends upon opposition. There are two ways opposition is important. First, opposition is necessary for individuals within groups to make choice. There needs to be clear alternatives: a this-or-that scenario, an either/or scenario, even a both/and scenario. Often the choices are not clear. A leadership task involves making the alternatives clearer to those who act to make them. In fact, confusing the issues, or being unclear about scenarios, information, or alternatives does not allow for people to make honest choices about real opposites. Using those confusion techniques takes real choice away from others and is merely a control technique.

I recall one senior manager of a small, start-up nonprofit organization who made it a point not to formalize or bureaucratize the systems and procedures used in the office. I asked him about this strategy and even offered to help formalize things, thinking that was a better way of running an office. He declined my help though. His rationale was that such formalization would limit his control and his capacity to be flexible because routine procedures and formality limit confusion and chaos. Standard operating procedures are just that: standard, unambiguous, certain. They ensure controlled behavior over time, but limit the discretion and individual control of an executive too. The nonprofit manager apparently wanted people *not* to know the answer, *not* to be able to act for themselves, so they would have to come to him for almost everything—what to do, how to interact, when to get things done, who to talk to, and so forth. He was in control. Contrary to that tactic, leadership recognizes that for collaboration to be real, the choice to collaborate must be able to be made with clear alternatives in mind. Confusion and obfuscation do not help in that process.

Second, opposition is necessary to know when a result of leadership—collaboration—is actually taking place. People find meaning and progress in collaboration only as they recognize that they are not in conflict with each other. The synergies of leadership are evident only by comparison to the lack of progress occurring in noncollaborative situations. So, even when people are collaborating, the principle of opposition is necessary for them to recognize that they are actually in collaboration and not in conflict.

Rules and Sanctions

Another element of individual choice is an acknowledgment that there are good consequences if certain choices are made and bad consequences if other choices are made. Defining this element requires us to believe that choices have consequences. Opposition offers alternatives; rules and laws offer us consequences. Those consequences are natural extensions of the choices. They are related and linked. For example, if I choose X, then Y will occur (and not Z). Certainly, many variations exist to define an X and a Y (and a Z), but the basic premise is that there are general laws or principles that apply to people and to social interactions, and following those laws yields the intended benefits. Revolting against those laws yields attendant punishments or negative, contrary results. These laws can be general, even universal, or they can be specific rules we create within different groups.

Certainly, we have seen this play out in the scandals of business and government organizations. For example, a business that follows the general principle of honesty in their accounting practices reaps the benefits of a good reputation and continued business. A business that "cooks the books" may reap short-term benefits, but over time the results are scandal, legal trouble, and ultimately the doors closing on the business. Beyond the business impacts, we have to realize that dishonesty in business practices also has personal impacts. Results of breaking the rules can be seen in schisms between people, low self-esteem, negative comparisons of the worth of people, unhealthy competition, deceit, confusion, sadness, the suppression of skills and talents, and a host of other potential relationship issues. Therefore an act of leadership is making clear for everyone what the rules and laws are *and* the attendant rewards and punishments that occur from keeping or breaking them. In essence, leaders help us know what we do and don't do in our collective activity. Understanding and teaching the rule and the potential advantages or disadvantages of following that rule or not is an activity of leadership. It allows people to freely choose and to act responsibly.

Recognition of Moral Rights and Moral Wrongs

To make a choice, there must also be a sense of what correct action is. We need to have a sense that we are able to discern the better alternatives that yield the better results. Here is where a sense of right and wrong needs to be in place for true leadership to unfold. Leadership and the attendant meaningful collaboration it creates must emerge from right choices that intend to lead to good things made by individual members over time. Integrity and trustworthiness—long-established values in leadership literature—make no sense if there is not a right and wrong way of interacting. Leadership is about discerning the right and the wrong in our values sets and encouraging and persuading the right choice consistently and enduringly. Such discernment and choice allow for freely chosen collaboration to retain its power and functionality. Choosing to join for the wrong reasons (meaning reasons that are wrong) results in disingenuousness and mistrust soon follows (almost as a natural consequences)—and then the collaboration is on its way to disintegration.

Protected Freedom to Choose

Fundamentally, the ability to choose has to be protected. Leadership, therefore, ensures in structure, in word, in deed, and in philosophy that choice is a part of the relationships developed. When there is no choice present in the relationship, something other than leadership is probably occurring, be it manipulation, control, domination, or the like. The piercing allegory of the Grand Inquisitor in Dostoevsky's *Crime and Punishment* explores the key role of freedom in society and the interesting consequences of engaging in a "leadership" that limits and destroys personal freedom, though perhaps ensuring personal security.

The Grand Inquisitor states, "Nothing is more seductive for man than his freedom of conscience, but nothing is a greater cause of suffering." Thus he plants the seed for rationalizing the destruction of freedom itself. He knows that free will and choice are the foundation of individual progress, but he hints to his interviewee that people really don't want to pay the price of that freedom. That price is the potential for hard times, suffering, difficult situations, and the need for personal responsibility. He suggests that free choice is not a practical foundation upon which to build a society or the collective action within society because it is, frankly, hard and difficult and can lead to sadness. Above all else, he suggests, people only want to be secure (that is, safe from difficulties) and happy (that is, free from pain and suffering).

The antidote to human suffering, according to the Inquisitor, is to make sure individuals have no choice or are unaware of choice at all. Ignorance is the key. For the Grand Inquisitor, ignorance of opposition, ignorance of consequences, and ignorance of moral rights and wrongs is the key to human success. In essence, he is saying that we should withhold the elements of choice stated above to protect people from themselves. If the Inquisitor has his way, all humankind will live and die happily in ignorance. He will lead them only to "death and destruction," but they will be happy and secure along the way. He offers this summary of his plan to destroy choice: "I tell Thee that man is tormented by no greater anxiety than to find someone quickly to whom he can hand over that gift of freedom with which the ill-fated creature is born. But only one who can appease their conscience can take over their freedom." For this reason, so-called leaders of the world have often tried to supply the wants and create (and fulfill) the needs for their followers—acting upon them—instead of allowing individuals to responsibly choose their own paths. The Grand Inquisitor offers a sophisticated fake of what real leadership is.

Leaders, to be real leaders, foster the environment for the four elements of choice listed above to exist. More specifically, leadership is the act of placing in the foreground the opportunity and requirements for choices to be made. Leadership is the bringing up of choices and the encouragement of some choices over others. All choices lead to consequences that are necessary follow-ons to the choices (meaning they naturally follow). Some consequences ensure the possibility that individuals have choices in the future, and this insurance is a hallmark of leadership. Some consequences preclude the possibility that individuals have choices in the future, and these are the hallmarks of control, oppression, and coercion.

In other words, true leadership depends on the free choice of individuals and encourages their continued free choice. The leader's toolbox is full of persuasion, values, visions, stories, narratives, explanations, inspirations, plans, hopes, aspirations, principles, trust, shared power, and the like. All of these are used to encourage the uniting of individuals to a common purpose. The true leader never has access to manipulation, coercion, trickery, fraud, or delusion. Such tools are used to compel individuals to conform and limit real choice because over time they disallow individuals from really choosing from among real, clear, possible alternatives.

To summarize this section, leadership is about leader and led working together from a common vantage point, while encouraging freedom of choice and actions, to accomplish what leader and led can both agree is beneficial. There is a strong element of collaboration in the ideas of leadership; there is a strong element of control in the ideas of management. Thus leadership is essentially a collaborative endeavor.

Individual Choice: The Normative

There is a more normative defense of choice as a leadership element as well. An organization, a system of government, a social governance structure, a collective engagement, or the like that dismisses the individual and aggrandizes and raises the profile and moral standing of the group or collective is an organizing system that potentially dismisses the rights, roles, and free choice of the individual. This happens because the group sees little value in them; they simply see the importance of the group. Although such leadership can make policies, programs, and decisions in the body politic, the society itself is less than normatively preferred if the protection and encouragement of *individual* rights, liberties, and expressions are not in the forefront of how collective efforts function. All too often, group rights are supported rather than individual rights.

This preference for group rights inevitably diminishes the individual as merely an element of the group without the same moral stature as the group itself. Put differently, the notion of the individual must always be on the mind of those engaged in civic activity, or the individual may be subsumed under the grandeur of activity for the greater good. Subsuming the individual might cause the collective will to overshadow and ignore (even oppose) the protection and encouragement, of individual flourishing, growth, and freedom of choice.

When the collective that forms through collaborative leadership assumes a greater normative stance than the individual choices that were essential for the formation of that collective, we run the distinct possibility of diminishing individual choice by our activities of collaborative leadership. Diminishing individual choice can cause society to be constituted not by individuals with free choice, values, and capacities but rather by group interests, group rights, and group-sustaining norms. Such a condition allows for groups to act upon individuals (meaning exert forces that minimize or ignore individual choice) for the good of the whole and in favor of individual uniformity and conformity to the whole. Acting upon others to encourage uniformity eliminates not only the opportunity but eventually the capacity of individuals to act for themselves.

A society made up of group interests protecting group rights acting upon individuals to encourage conformity and uniformity is not, I argue, normatively preferred to a society or organization made up of individuals protecting the individual's right to act for him or herself and to choose to join together with others in substantive and useful colabor with a sense of common purpose and unity. The distinction is important. Individuals choosing to act in ways that cause them to join in unified purpose does not necessitate the diminishing of the individual, but rather the opposite. Such choice requires the focus on *people* making *individual* choices. Those choices to join together encompass issues that often require the nobler characteristics of individuals: humility, wisdom, sacrifice, love, altruism, patience, reason, trust, trustworthiness, and ennobled and disciplined self-interest.

When individuals are acted upon by the group to encourage the interests of the group despite the wishes of individuals, then the individual becomes diminished, and even disregarded and dismissed. A society of individuals who are dismissed and ignored is not a society where people flourish, grow, and enjoy freedom. No state where groups flourish but people do not can compare. Such a state is normatively less desirable. Collaborative leadership, while envisioning diverse, power-sharing groups working together, can never encourage the groups to overshadow the individuals within them.

So as we encourage and develop further capacity in leadership activities, let us not forget that when we work together, the unit of analysis is, both practically and normatively, the individual and not the resultant collective. The individual has to be the unit of analysis as voice teaches us that one of the main concerns is not only to clarify and express our voice, but to help others individually clarify and express their own voices. Many leadership writers, like Stephen Covey in his book *The 8th Habit*, have suggested that "once you've found your own voice, the *choice* to expand your influence, to increase your contribution, is the choice to inspire others to find *their* voice."[1] Certainly, as we share or come to share a common voice, leadership is present, but it is present only if we have freely chosen to share or come to share that voice.

Sense of Self

Perhaps obviously, one of the most important individuals to consider in the leadership phenomenon is you, yourself. Most of what we know about leadership is focused on others. We serve others within the values, vision, and vectors we come to share together. The relationship with others is of key concern, and of course we recognize that leadership itself is best defined and determined by looking at the followers, not ourselves, per se. However, at this point, it is time to focus on our own sense of ourselves. As we speak of voice in terms of choice, volition, and volunteerism, we need to also speak of voice in terms of our own voice speaking forth our own sense of who we are.

Voice is shorthand for giving place in our work for our authentic selves to stand tall and be counted. To be authentic we must understand who we are inside and out. In doing so we are humble enough to acknowledge our weaknesses and we can see our strengths for what they really are. Authentic voice asks us to lead ourselves. Bruce Avolio, the director of the Gallup Leadership Institute and a pioneer in research about authentic leadership, combines with his colleagues to conclude that leaders who are authentic and who voice that authenticity are characterized by these types of things: they "a) know who they are and what they believe in; b) display transparency and consistency between their values, ethical reasoning, and actions; c) focus on developing positive psychological states such as confidence, optimism, hope, and resilience within themselves and their associates; d) are widely known and respected for their integrity."[2]

Certainly, leading ourselves is essential. The notion of voice helps us know why it's important. We have defined earlier the idea of choice and its absolutely pivotal role in leadership. In so doing, we talked a lot about followers choosing to follow and allowing that choice to exist. We briefly mentioned that leaders choose to lead too.

I will say that some people choose to follow people who themselves didn't know they were being followed and may not have chosen consciously to lead anyone. But for our purposes, leaders who want to lead make a choice. We discussed choice already, but let's turn our attention to looking inward, looking at ourselves as we engage in leadership. First, we will look at letting others know who we are and what we believe in; then, we will try to make sure we aren't fooling ourselves.

Articulating One's Own Voice

Before we can get others to follow our values and vision, we must know what our values and vision are. We need to be clear in our own mind before we can inspire the hearts and minds of others. This is not a new idea. Perhaps you have already heard these or similar statements: "We cannot light a fire in others until it is lit in us." "You can't pull people up to new heights if you aren't there already." "You cannot inspire others until you are first inspired." Making sure what you communicate is consistent with who you are and what you believe in is the hallmark of effectively articulating your own voice. It's a powerful element of leadership. Part of the work of leading others is making sure you know where to lead them, or at least what values and principles you should teach others on your journey together. The real work of leadership is *inner* work. The work done inside of you is the genesis of the work of leadership that people see on the outside. We must be clear what our values are and will be. It is okay to work a little bit on the vision and vectors, but we must be clear for sure on our values. Although we discussed values already, we can add in this chapter that being clear on your personal values and the values you want to engage with in whatever joint activity you may lead is a prerequisite for leadership. A personal discovery of yourself is a necessary precondition to your leadership. Here are two simple, time-tested ways to find out what you really believe and what is really important to you.

The first method to discovering what you value is by experiencing the writing of your own obituary, or, if you prefer fewer words, your own epitaph. For instance, what can we learn from the epitaph of Thomas Jefferson, which he prepared for himself: "Here was buried Thomas Jefferson Author of the Declaration of American Independence of the Statute of Virginia for religious freedom & Father of the University of Virginia"? Certainly, we can learn what seemed important to him. We learn his accomplishments, yes, but when we learn the areas of his accomplishments and what he focused on in his life, we learn even more about the person. In other words, what he wrote in his epitaph summarizes what he felt was important in his life. Parenthetically, it would be a good thing (a very good thing) to know what is important in *our* lives.

Susan B. Anthony's epitaph summarizes a lifetime of effort and the values that undergirded them: "Liberty, Humanity, Justice, Equality." Though written by someone else, George Washington Carver's epitaph says something of his character and the reasons for his profound influence: "He could have added fortune to fame, but caring for neither, he found happiness and honor in being helpful to the world."

From these few examples, you can see that summarizing one's life into the essentials is a task of serious introspection. It requires clarity of values and a true sense of purpose. It requires a public declaration of a lifetime of decisions and the criteria for those decisions. It allows for the principles that guided your life's purpose to be explained to others, even to those who have never known you. In that sense, you are doing what leadership requires: you are making known what you believe in or want to work toward so that others, even others who do not know you, may make an evaluation for themselves about your worthiness to be their leader. Writing an epitaph requires some editing for sure. Writing an obituary allows you to be a bit more verbose and capture a few more elements of what is really important to you. If you want a sense of who you really are, write down what you have spent your life doing.

Another activity to help us gain clarity about ourselves is to create your personal coat of arms. Used in the Middle Ages, a coat of arms identified and distinguished individuals. In British heraldry, coats of arms were individual, not familial. It truly was about you. It was a symbol of the individual who wore one. There are different elements of a coat of arms, including the shield, the field, the mantling, the helm, the crest, and so forth. The colors themselves had symbolic value. The motto, if any, also had literal value of what the person held as important.

Applying a coat of arms to yourself today requires much the same introspection as in days of yore. You have to think about what is important to you and what you want to be known for or known to be like. Translating these personal values and attributes into symbolic elements of a coat of arms is an interesting way to gain clarity about what you are all about. It has the added benefit of allowing others to see (quite literally) what you are all about as they look upon the coat of arms and its accompanying symbols.

A brief review of the parts of a coat of arms is probably required at this point. Figure 5.1 shows a make-believe coat of arms. Claiming no expertise in heraldry, I can still provide some generic definitions that would be helpful. The *shield* is the most identifiable part. Its shape can differ and is usually an indication of geography; the shape is simply a reflection of

FIGURE 5.1. Elements of a Coat of Arms

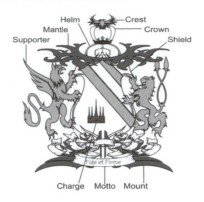

individual preference. Dividing the shield has its formal procedures and even symbolic purposes, as do the colors, designs, symbols, and *charges*, if any. A *helm* may be added above the shield and is simply a depiction of a helmet. A wreath or crown may be added atop a helm, but usually above the helmet is some design, animal, or plumage, which is called the *crest*. A *motto* may be placed floating above the crest or at the bottom of the shield and is determined by personal preference. On either side of the shield is sometimes found what is called the *mantle* or *mantling*, usually a plumage or leaf design. Outside of the mantling are what is called *supporters*, depictions of people, animals, or birds. Below the shield may be placed a name, though the placement, design, and typeset are all determined by preference. The entire design is often placed on a *mount*, which grounds it. Colors, designs, symbols, creatures, and the like all have symbolic value in coats of arms. It is this symbolism that is most useful in helping us recognize what we value and stand for: in other words, what we are all about.

Whether or not anyone sees our personal coat of arms or reads our self-prepared obituary or epitaph, going through the introspection necessary to create such things is the real key. Knowing ourselves and articulating that knowledge to ourselves and to others is a leadership activity. We cannot inspire others unless we are inspiring. It is a leadership task to know what makes us tick, to know the values we breathe in and live out day to day.

Avoiding Self-Deception

With all the introspection required to both know and articulate one's voice, we have to make sure we aren't kidding ourselves. An idea I have found useful comes from the Arbinger Institute. It is the notion of self-deception.[3] Self-deception is the problem of not knowing one's own role in the problems we complain about. It is the lack of acknowledgment (and associated actions) that I might have some role to play in the creation or escalation of the problems I focus on and grumble about.

Think for a moment about the most difficult people you have had to work with. What were their issues? Why was it hard to work for them? What were they like? After you have listed all of their faults and issues, ask yourself whether they thought they were a problem the way you thought they were a problem. If you are like most people I talk to about this, your answer is no: those hard-to-work-with people had no clue they were a problem, but you (and everyone) else knew. Those people suffer from self-deception. They are unable to see that they play a role in the problems of the organization or their relationships. Of course, the conclusion about those hard-to-work-with people can also be turned toward us; we may be self-deceived too.

This idea of self-deception is clearer as you talk about a specific problem, like low morale, or poor communication, or inept management skills. Let's pick poor communication in the office as our problem and see how self-deception might work. The boss (and everyone else) is complaining that there is poor communication and wants to fix it. He lays out a plan, sends people to training, hires a consultant, and institutes many other activities that are designed to fix the problem of poor communication among employees. But nothing seems to work.

The notion of self-deception teaches us that the reason there is no real solution is that we may not have dealt with the real problem. Poor communication in the office may merely be a symptom of the real problem that the boss is self-deceived in thinking he has, for example, an open-door policy when he really doesn't. The boss may be self-deceived that he takes time to explain issues to his subordinates, but in fact he does not. His employees have spent months, even years, complaining that he never listens to suggestions, has no time to meet with them, and never clearly explains what he wants. Until the boss comes to grip with his own self-deception, and deals with his own role in creating and escalating the problem of poor communication, the problem will remain unresolved. Although the real problem is the boss's self-deception, he will continue to work on the symptom of that self-deception: poor communication.

Speaking of communication, I recall a story told about a father who felt he didn't have the quality communication he hoped for with his teenage son. Interestingly, the father summed up the problem by saying, "That boy never listens to me." What a profound, yet very subtle, admission of self-deception. What the father wanted was quality communication, but what he demanded was that his son listen to him. There was no indication that the father was willing to listen to his son. To the father, good communication meant that the son listens. And the son, just wanting to be heard once in a while, eventually gave up and tuned out. If only the father could have overcome his self-deception and realized that the lack of communication was a symptom of the real problem of his own unwillingness to listen. Then the communication would have improved dramatically.

In much of the discussion of self-deception's impact on people and organization, we recognize that it takes two to tango. In other words, the son may be self-deceived as well as the father. The employees in the office with poor communication may also be self-deceived. Often people engaged in collective action collude with each other to continue their own self-deceptions. In this context, collusion is when two or more people are self-deceived and blame each other for the problems they complain about. They thereby provide each other with the justification for their own self-deceived behaviors, thus never resolving the problems. The son may feel that he does listen to his father, when indeed he doesn't. The employees may think they are cooperative and nice, when in reality they consistently give the boss a hard time and never engage with him even when he tries.

The truth is we reveal ourselves in the way we see and treat others. There is enough blame to go around, but the little secret of self-deception is that we can stop this collusion, and we can actually engage genuinely with others. We simply have to look to ourselves first, rather than see problems only in others.

I remember what a wise man once said about this idea of self-deception, though such a formal concept was foreign to him. He had just discerned it on his own (perhaps that is what made him wise). He said in essence that when someone talks badly or complains about him, the first thing he does is look inside himself trying to remind himself of the interactions with others or simply his actions in general, to try to find the seed of behavior that could have been misunderstood or taken in such a way that it could grow into the tree of discontent. Then he tries to fix that seed. Either he throws that seed away from his life, or he plants it in different soil so it grows differently. He sees what he might have done to cause that person to feel that way about him and he fixes himself, because he concludes he has a hard time fixing others.

That kind of humility, introspection, and personal quest for improvement is a hallmark of leadership and part of this thing we call *voice*. For those of us who aren't quite there yet, here are three telling signs that we might be self-deceived:

- *It becomes difficult for us to "do right" because we don't allow any conflict with our own inclinations.* What we are inclined to think is "the one right way" may in fact not be.
- *We have an irrational optimism that no matter what we do, there will be a happy ending.* Happy endings are good goals, but not every action we take will necessarily lead to them.
- *We prompt ourselves to think of ourselves only in the highest terms, regardless of what we may actually do.* Our sense of self must be tempered by a humility that overpowers pride.

If these kinds of attitudes are found in us, we need to work on our own self-deception. We need to focus on the underlying causes of problems (often found in personal foibles and interactions) rather than on the surface symptoms individually. We need to stop thinking that our problems are always caused by something outside of ourselves. Maybe, just maybe, we have a role to play in the problems we complain about. We need to recognize, especially as leaders, that our influence is based on our ability to be genuine in our attitudes toward ourselves, toward our situation, and toward others. Only by taking responsibility for our problems can we solve them. We need to ask ourselves, ultimately, if we are willing to expose ourselves to ourselves. As we do these kinds of things, our voice increases in confidence, fidelity with our actions, and influence. Overcoming self-deception allows us to be able to be and act in ways that leadership intends.

To Act or Be Acted Upon: The Primacy of Agency

If we don't overcome self-deception, we may never be fully able to act for ourselves. Instead, our own follies will act upon us. Again the questions of acting for ourselves or being acted upon by others emerge as we discuss leadership. It is a fundamental question, a defining dimension of leadership. Not only should we help others act for themselves and avoid the temptation to act upon them, leadership requires that we learn to act for ourselves—genuinely and faithfully consistent with our guiding values and principles—and avoid being acted upon by personal peccadilloes, pride, or circumstance.

I remember witnessing a scene that reinforces leadership as an endeavor that honors agency while encouraging moral choices. A little boy had just walked through a museum gift shop but was uncharacteristically quiet. The parents, with a total of four children in tow, were pleased they escaped the gift shop without having bought anything. However, the mother noticed the boy's expression and behavior and asked if something was wrong. With the intuition mothers seem to have, she asked the right questions and learned the boy had taken a candy bar. No one had paid for it. The father entered the picture with obvious unhappiness and stern concern, but he had enough wisdom to see that Mom had this one.

Though reasoning with young children has its limitations, she was able to explain in simple terms that there are consequences to such actions. The mother talked with the boy in terms he could understand, but she was thoughtful and focused in her simple conversation. She explained that all choices have consequences. She explained the consequences of this particular choice—to the store owner, to law and order, and more importantly to the boy's character. The boy confessed he was hungry. Mom explained that we often have to delay the gratification of our desires.

Then Mom did what I thought was a wonderful example of leadership. She explained that the boy now had another choice to make and discussed some of the consequences of that choice. The boy had to choose what to do to make things right. Ultimately, the boy chose to talk with the store manager (with Mom's help), confess what he did, give the candy bar back, and pay for it anyway out of the little money he had. The store owner thought this was too much, but the boy stood firm, and the mom let him stand by his choice. As the boy walked out of the store, he had a strangely happy look on his face. You could tell he was still hungry, but he was pleased with how he felt. It was almost as if he could tell his character had just grown in good ways.

To me, choice and consequences were the essence of this scene. The boy made choices. Consequences followed. The mom made choices to help the boy make choices. She didn't act upon the boy to cause him to do what she knew was right. Rather, she encouraged the boy to act for himself in ways he was becoming to know was right.

We are all moral agents. A *moral agent* is a human being capable of acting with respect to what is right and wrong, while the consequences of those choices and actions are not necessarily in his control but follow from the morality of the choices and actions. Leadership encourages the use of that freedom to choose as people decide to engage in collective activities.

Leadership asks that we ourselves, we who choose to lead, use that freedom of choice to act in accordance with what we know to be true, good, and beautiful. It asks us to have integrity, showing by word and deed the integration found within ourselves of what we know to be true, and acting according to what the truth demands. In this way, we maintain the freedom to choose (our agency) as we resist the forces that try to act upon us to either limit our choices or diminish who were really are. With such a focus, our leadership is both formed and informed by our voice.

Points to Ponder

1. In what ways is leadership a voluntary activity? What do leaders and followers volunteer to do?
2. On what basis do you choose your leaders? Why do you choose to follow some people and not others?
3. How might an organization of volunteers differ from a typically managed for-profit organization? Could a for-profit organization survive if it treated its members as if they were volunteers rather than salaried employees? Why or why not?
4. What are the four general elements or conditions of real choice? How might leaders ensure and encourage these conditions?
5. Why might leadership be more about individual choice and individual rights, even though the results of leadership revolve around groups and collective activity?
6. How does a real sense of oneself relate to leadership? In other words, how does your inner voice impact leadership?
7. How have you experienced self-deception in your life? How can a diligent effort to avoid self-deception change or impact the way you might engage with others and do leadership?
8. What does it mean to be able to act for yourself? What does it mean to be acted upon by others or by external forces?

Quotables

1. "Liberty, according to my metaphysics is a self-determining power in an intellectual agent. It implies thought and choice and power." —John Adams, U.S. president and founding father
2. "When the conduct of men is designed to be influenced, persuasion, kind, unassuming persuasion, should ever be adopted. It is an old and a true maxim, that a drop of honey catches more flies than a gallon of gall." —Abraham Lincoln, U.S. president

Practical Activities

1. *Knowing Yourself.* A sense of self requires of us to look inside and determine what we really care about, what we really exert effort to accomplish, and what we really value. With that sense of self, our inner voice becomes a powerful partner in leading others and valuing the concept of voice in the leadership relationship. To help in this process, prepare one or two examples of your personal epitaph. Keep the epitaph to no more than 10 to 20 words. Your epitaph should include the things you would like to be known for or a summary of the things you stood for in life. After the epitaph is prepared, use it as a foundation to expand your summary into a full-page obituary. This will allow you to explain what you meant in the epitaph or include more details about what is important to you.

2. *Personal Coat of Arms.* Design and draw your coat of arms. There are a number of resources online or in print that clarify the meaning of the symbols and styles of a traditional coat of arms. Review them, and then choose the elements that align with your sense of self. Your personal crest should include things that are important to you, elements of your personality (or what you want it to be), your accomplishments, your lifelong commitments, and so forth. Share this coat of arms with people who know you and note their reactions. Modify your coat of arms over time if needed.

3. *Remembering Your Choices.* Make an effort to think about past experiences when you made choices, even difficult choices, staying true to your values. Discern what precipitated the choice. Decide whether others tried to act upon you to make one choice over another and whether you gave in to such pressure or stayed firm to your values or preferences. Write down how you felt before, during, and after the choice and the benefits and costs of being a moral agent. Write down how this experience may influence your leadership of others.

Notes

1. Stephen R. Covey, *The 8th Habit: From Effectiveness to Greatness* (New York: Free Press, 2004), 31.

2. Bruce J. Avolio, William L. Gardner, and Fredo O. Walumbwa, "Preface," in *Authentic Leadership Theory and Practice: Origins, Effects and Development*, Vol. 3, eds. William L. Gardner, Bruce J. Avolio, and Fredo O. Walumbwa (San Diego, CA: Elsevier, 2005), xxiii.

3. For more information see Arbinger Institute, *Leadership and Self Deception: Getting out of the Box, 2nd Edition* (San Francisco: Berret-Koehler, 2010).

Chapter 6

Strategic Thinking and Planning Process: Using the Four Vs

The Four Vs framework is a powerful diagnostic tool. It helps us figure out the leadership other people are doing. This framework gives us information as to whether or not they are doing leadership at all and whether or not we would choose to follow. It also helps us know what we have to work on (our strategies and tasks) as we choose to follow. It gives us the elements of leadership we must engage in to do the leadership we want to do. In some sense, the framework is philosophical, but it is also highly practical. One way it can be practical for us is in the world of strategic planning and thinking.

In the discussion of vectors, we mentioned that there is a difference between the *how* plans of traditional strategic planning (what some have labeled strategic programming) and the addition of the *why/what* elements of what is being called strategic thinking. Defining the context as more than a mere scan of the environment, strategic thinking asks us to couple strategic planning with an understanding of the leadership context of the work being done, the relational aspects, the meaning making, and the values and vision connections of our work. In chapter 4 we highlighted the following ideas to help us think as we plan:

- Adopt a values, vision, and vector orientation rather than a goals, objectives, metrics mentality.
- See yourself as an organizational philosopher more than as a technical expert.
- Concentrate on the flow of information and the quality of relationships that emerge rather than the control of information.
- Learn to accept and work with ambiguity and the qualitative nature of organizations, rather than try to control and quantify all organizational endeavors.

FIGURE 6.1. The STP Process

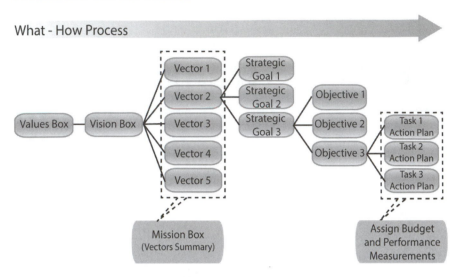

These ideas help us remember that *what* and *how* we do things in an organization are much more appropriate and meaningful if they are informed by *why* doing them the way we do is important organizationally and personally; the why we do what we do helps us fulfill the values, vision, and raison d'être of the organization.

The Four Vs offer an easy formula for linking the thinking with the planning and the doing. In this chapter, we will review this Four Vs framework of strategic thinking/planning—what we will call STP for short. Visually, this framework looks something like Figure 6.1. It helps us see how to link strategic thinking about who we are and why we should do certain things and not others to the tactical actions that help us actually get the things done. Figure 6.1 represents the "connectivity" that can be established between the components of STP. Seeing and creating connections between these components of thinking and planning is central to strategic thinking and leadership.

The STP Process

We will define each box in the figure and then describe the simple methodology used to fill in each box. To engage in the STP process, we must first clarify the values that serve to define who we are and define the decision criteria we use to decide what we should do.

Values Box

Values occupies the first box. As mentioned in chapter 2, values play a central role in the leadership relationship. They guide our behavior both individually and organizationally. They impact how we see the world. They serve as decision criteria for the choices we face in life and in organizations. Values are the currency of the leader-follower relationship. As such leaders are clear on their own values, but they also recognize the need to impact the values of potential followers.

Therefore leaders must be comfortable with a values connotation in the work they do, because leaders and followers depend upon them. Whether they plan it or not, leaders share their values with followers through their actions even if they don't share them through words. In like manner so do the actions of the organization. Organizations have values, decision criteria, and core beliefs that guide their overall activities. Although some of these are explicit, they are always implicit; they are always there. As you prepare to fill in this box, the following questions may be helpful:

- Do I recognize that people have values and that those values trigger behavior? Do I recognize that people bring their values to work?
- As I try to shape what others in the office are doing, have I given enough emphasis on shaping their values?
- Do I have a clear sense of my own values?
- Have I devoted enough time to understanding the organizational and personal values at work in my office?
- What role do values play in going from strategic thinking to strategic planning?

Begin the STP process by asking yourself and the organization (or the group assembled from the organization) what is important to or valuable about the organization. What is it that makes this organization look or feel different from another organization? What are the organizational values as the members see them? This should be an individual activity at first. Having people write down these values separately allows for three things: an honest assessment of values without the fear of peer pressure; a potentially long list of values to work with; and lastly, a potential for convergence of values, or rather the potential for obviously similar values from multiple people. The eventual convergence of values that emerges strengthens the evidence of a real organizational values set. Once these values are listed together for all to see, there needs to be a process to focus on the few (say four to seven) values that are strongest and most indicative of the organization. Techniques to do that will be discussed a little later.

One group using this technique came up with a solid list of values. The group thought their work expressed a good summary list of generic values: professionalism, accuracy, customer service, integrity, honesty, fairness, and so forth. However, as they discussed the values and engaged in a process to narrow them down, define them, and refine them, an interesting phenomenon happened. They developed different, more user-friendly, more accurate values that really drive their work every day, values they really bought into because they reflected what they really valued, not simply what sounded good or had been previously outlined as the organization's values. Gone was the generic list of corporate values, replaced by a list of the real, energizing values specific to the collective activity they were doing.

Making the formal lists and working a process to narrow the values down by discussing them are essential steps in discerning what is really important—what really drives the work and inspires the people. Instead of previously stated, rather generic values, the group mentioned above ended up with these values: ease (of interactions), reliability (of systems, processes, and people), partnerships (within and outside the organization), and return on investment (in an increased ability to provide services). Perhaps these aren't the values for your organization. They weren't originally even the stated values of that organization. But through thinking and discussing together, they became the values outlining what they really cared about and what they wanted to continue to be as an organization. As you engage the process of clarifying your organization's values, you also will see a values set emerge that is more specific, more useful, and more accurately descriptive of your organization. A list of values like that will serve your organization much better than a list of generic values we metaphorically take off the "values shelf" and try to shoehorn into our organizations.

Once this "real" list is finalized, there is a good set of values from which other decisions can be made. This is an important point. Throughout the STP process, decisions have to be made among differing opinions and ideas. Clarifying what is really important to the organization is the ultimate means by which these differences can be resolved. *Values serve as decision criteria*, and as decisions are made based on the values, the values themselves become refined and more user-friendly.

Vision Box

One of the greatest challenges of leadership is to create a shared focus around what to do, and why we do it, and how (both the means and the ethics) we continue to do it despite the changing environments around us. Leadership demands that we help others see how our values play out. This is an activity of creating a shared reality about the organization and the means to align people with the organization's purposes.

In the absence of a shared focus (or vision), people interpret things on their own, being pulled by various potential values and pressures, or various definitions of the same values. In essence, they create their own what, why, and how. These various creations can lead to work occurring at cross-purposes to what the organization is or to what a leader is looking to do. Unless people can align their perspectives to the focus of the group, they may not see how their efforts connect to other people's efforts, and they may never achieve the satisfaction of knowing how their work contributes to the greater whole.

Leaders have always needed to create alignment or a common focus among people who are required or choose to work together. This ability is especially important in today's organizational climate, where individuals often shift from one team or project to another and where their tasks are not routine but change according to the services being rendered. Once people in a group achieve common understanding and acceptance of the vision, they can pursue shared goals almost completely autonomously. Being aligned and sharing in the vision, they work on what is important, in ways that are consistent with the overall purpose and essence of the group—even when things are ambiguous or chaotic.

Aligning values into a vitalizing vision is central to doing leadership in an organization. In a sense, a vision encompasses both the present and the future core values of followers. Vision stories or statements are how leaders communicate the vision to followers; it is a part of the visioning process. As leaders, we must recognize our vision-setting role. These questions may help you prepare for this role:

- How do you fulfill your values?
- Are there elements of what, why, and how that change over time? How does that change affect the aligning vision?
- What is the relative importance of each value for you? Does that importance impact how you articulate the vision and how others may receive it?
- What kind of story can you express that captures the essence of your vision?
- How does the vision relate to the idea of culture?
- What differentiates your organization from other organizations?

All this talk of alignment is basically the notion of making sure your vision articulates how the organization and the people in it can fulfill the values that are important (and agreed upon). Remember, visions operationalize values.

A good way to develop a vision is to develop a vision story. Simply ask people to write down a short depiction of how they see the values playing out as they do their work. Or have them write a scenario about how the values are linked together to illustrate what the organization is all about.

Over the years, I have been surprised at how similar the stories and scenarios are. Sharing the stories with each other and then highlighting the commonalities among them begin to shape a summary view, an edited vision story, that can form the foundation of current and future action. Once that vision is known and shared, people begin to want to work in ways that make it true and active in day-to-day work processes and activities. They know how to align themselves to the values and vision because they have a picture of what it is all about. That vision, that picture, is a profound tool used to unite and align individuals in collective work.

Of course a vision statement can be developed too. Such a statement should reflect the values of the organization and be shorthand for who we are and what we can become because of who we are. As an example, the following vision statement is an attempt to shorthand the final values of the organization discussed in the Values Box section above (though I will modify it to cloak the organization's identity): *We partner with others to provide easy, reliable [service the group provides].* Coupled with the vision story they created, the workers in the organization have a sense of how the work they do aligns with the values they hold dear.

Vectors and a Vector Summary (Mission) Box

Vectors are the nuts and bolts of vision. They help us know what we are to do specifically and distinctly to make our vision a reality. They are related to the general notion of missions. In fact, if you develop three or four vector phrases and then link them together with semicolons, you come up with what might be known as a mission statement. Again, supporting the organization's vision is the primary mission of every organization. However, to provide some detail, an organization's "mission" is the things it does to reinforce the reason it exists. An organization's mission is the stuff they do to provide "value" to society, its shareholders and/or stakeholders, its customers, and its employees. The organization's mission is its primary support function. It is what the organization does and/or provides that is unique to that organization and makes it competitive within its niche. Missions help us know what the organization accomplishes, its "value-added" work. They help us know what we don't do as well. Missions give us a feel for the day-to-day work and how it is linked to the values and vision. If a "sense of mission" is perceived as lacking or no longer meaningful, goals and objectives may have little meaning for the organization. Mission should tie goals to vision and reinforce the value orientation of the culture. It should help the organization understand who it is and what it does. These questions may help:

- What vectors make sense to accomplish your vision? Can you summarize them into a vector summary or mission statement?
- Does your organization already have a formal or informal mission statement? Is it still relevant?
- Is there more than one mission in your organization? How do you know? What vectors provides the focus?
- What role do mission and vectors play in going from strategic thinking to strategic planning?

The Four Vs framework reminds us that missions are really just summaries of the vectors we have developed to accomplish our vision. We will discuss a technique to determine these vectors a little later. What is important to realize about these mission and vectors boxes is that they mark the transition from thinking to doing. It is here in the STP figure (see Figure 6.2) that leadership and management overlap. It is here where the work of linkage and relationship and creativity are merged with the work of outlining the tasks of work.

FIGURE 6.2. Leadership, Management, and the STP Process

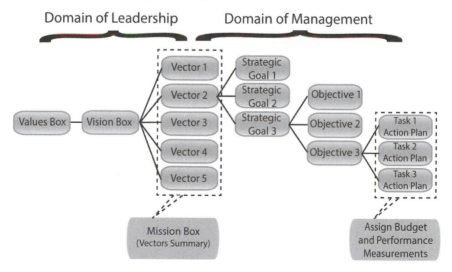

As an example of vectors, the organization (whose values and vision we already shared above) determined the following vectors: Enhance Technology Initiatives; Invest in Employees; Impact the Legislative and Regulatory Environment; Organize and Maintain Partnerships; Ensure Organizational Learning. The mission statement they created looks something like this: "We partner with others to provide easy, reliable [work that it does] in a way that enhances technological solutions, streamlines the legislative and regulatory environment, develops and maintains partnerships, ensures organizational learning, and invests in the people who do the work."

This is not a statement for every organization; nevertheless, such a statement is an example of mission statements (vector summaries) linked to the vision and values and that point the way to developing strategic goals that implement the vectors. The mission outlines the work focus, the key results anticipated, and essential elements that differentiate them from other organizations, at least for now. All of their current work fits underneath one of those vectors, and future work will as well.

Long-Term Strategic Goals Box

The task of making vectors a reality is what traditional strategic planning has been about. The task of outlining long-term goals to accomplish the mission has long been a function of management. Essentially, these long-term goals provide a broad understanding of what the organization needs to accomplish in order to survive and/or thrive. They are few in number and reflect organizational targets that cause an inevitable flow of lower-order activities. These goals of three-to five-year duration come directly from the higher-order vectors, thereby providing direct linkage in terms of how priorities can drive goals. They should be measurable to allow for performance evaluations and strategic adjustments. These goals go by a variety of terms. We call these types of goals *strategic goals*, but the term means less than the actual concept.

Short-Term Goals and Objectives Box

Short-term goals flow from the long-term goals and should drive the day-to-day functions of the organization. These zero- to two-year goals should be specific, measurable, attainable, realistic, and time related. As such they serve to connect in real terms the strategy of higher-order goals to the tactics of everyday work tasks. Additionally, the management of short-term objectives provides the framework for an organization's annual business plan. Short-term objectives are articulated in well-defined action plans, tasks, budgets, and performance criteria.

TABLE 6.1. Example of Action Plan Chart

Action to Be Taken	Date to Be Completed	People Responsible	Method Used	Resources Needed	Special Needs

When we accomplish these objectives, we know we are working appropriately and moving the organization forward. Unless we are very focused as leaders and teach the thinking behind the tasks, and not just the tasks themselves, the average worker may not know anything about the organization beyond the specific short-term goal his or her work relates to. When that kind of myopia exists, it is hard for workers to feel connected, aligned, or inspired by the overall purpose of the organization. Rather, it is easy for workers to feel confused, poorly motivated, and frustrated.

Tasks and Action Plans Box

Where the rubber meets the road is where tasks and action plans exist. In very summary terms, an *action plan* is a way of making sure certain tasks are accomplished. Interestingly, as this action plan is worked through, additional tasks are determined as well. Basically, an action plan outlines the who and what and when and how much of the tasks needed to accomplish the articulated goals. It ensures the accomplishment of the solution (or tasks), and coordination of data collection.

A simple way to depict an action plan is by creating a chart that shows the plans in an organized way. The chart looks something like Table 6.1. Keep in mind that you need to put the plan into writing; don't worry about filling in the columns one at a time, in sequence. The parts of the action plan can be filled in any order and can be changed as circumstances and quality of work and workers change.

Putting It Together: A Deployment Process and "Tool Box"

Getting from the vision through the values, vision, and mission vectors to goals and objectives can be accomplished in a systematic way. By employing a small set of "process tools," we can connect the components of strategic thinking with a disciplined methodology to help align what people do with where the organization needs to go. The methodology uses *brain-storming*, *affinity analysis*, and *multivoting* to develop well-scoped and defined tasks, with a schedule, deliverables, and measures. This narrowing-down process can be used at any level of the STP, from values all the way to tasks, and is accomplished by using a "what-how" methodology.

It is this what-how methodology that allows us to think about the elements in broad terms with broad input and then narrow both the organization and the tasks into essential parts. We will begin using a vector as our starting point for illustration. Here are the steps:

1. Begin with a vector. Name that vector a *what*. Ask *how* we can accomplish the vector. Brainstorm a list of *hows*. Determine if any of the *hows* can be grouped into a general category because they are similar in content and intent. This grouping, called *affinity analysis*, reduces the number of *hows* to a more manageable list by finding items that have an affinity for each other, or rather, the ones that are like each other.

2. Use multivoting to reduce the list down to between one to five key *hows*. Multivoting is described below. By reducing the number of *hows* to five or so, people are able to both remember and begin to commit to the *hows*.

3. Work with one *how* at a time. This *how* we will now call a *what* and it will be more defined than the vector. It is one way the vector can be fulfilled. The list of *hows* is now composed of examples of the strategic goals discussed above. They are directly linked to the vector and will help us know whether the vector is accomplished, but they are also relatively broad in nature. We will have to figure out how to accomplish the strategic goal. Hence, what was a *how* is now a *what* in our minds, and the question becomes: how do we fulfill this particular strategic goal?

4. Repeat the brainstorming, affinity analysis, and multivoting for each strategic goal. The results (the final list of *hows*) are objectives under each strategic goal. Brainstorm a list of *hows*. Determine how the *hows* should be grouped (affinity analysis). Multivote the list down to one to five *hows*.

5. Work again with each *how* separately. A *how* now becomes a *what* and is more defined than the long-term strategic goals and is the basis for our objectives.

6. Repeat the brainstorming, affinity analysis, and multivoting. Brainstorm a list of *hows*. Determine how the *hows* should be grouped (affinity analysis). Multivote the list down to a few *hows*.

7. Work again with each *how* separately. This *how* now becomes a *what* and if actionable is a task. This *what* eventually achieves a level of detail that an action plan can be developed in terms of what, who, when, and how to get that thing done.

This process should be repeated for each grouping of vectors, strategic goals, objectives, and so forth until you reach a point where the *what* is actually the *how*. In other words, it is a doable, measurable task to be completed in some way. In this manner, you can actually see a flowchart of day-to-day tasks, linked to objectives, linked to strategic goals, linked to vectors, linked to vision, and ultimately linked to the values of the organization.

Creating from these activities a flowchart modeled after the STP figure will demonstrate how to maintain the connectivity of the "high ground" of values, vision, vectors, and strategic goals to the "on the ground" goals, objectives, and actionable tasks. From this, too, we will be able to see a way to budget for the overall activities of the organization. Brainstorming and multivoting are described in more detail below.

Brainstorming

Brainstorming is a technique for generating a list of ideas about an issue. It is used to generate lists of problems, topics for data collection, potential solutions, items to monitor, and the like. Brainstorming can be used anywhere you want multiple ideas and/or more group energy. Brainstorming is a way to put into practice the ideal of voice, allowing people to be heard in a safe environment.

This technique is not difficult in concept. Decide on a topic (such as "problem we face" or "solutions to problem X" or "ideas to fulfill the vision"). Have each member offer in turn an idea about the topic. It is often wise to have them write ideas on a separate piece of paper individually before they need to verbalize them to the group. This allows them to avoid peer pressure or editing their own comments as they begin to hear other group members' opinions. When the time comes to hear everyone's ideas, other members should refrain from any comment, listen carefully, and build on each other's ideas.

Have one person record all the ideas on a flip chart. It is best to use the person's own words (within the limits of flip chart paper) to capture the speaker's intent. Otherwise, the scribe gets to edit and even editorialize in capturing others' ideas, which limits the safety-of-ideas zone intended by the technique. Continue the process until the team feels it has exhausted its ideas on the topic. Discuss and clarify the ideas on the list. Table 6.2 illustrates the results of this process.

Keep in mind these basic ground rules, which will help get the most out of the brainstorming session. Set a time limit for the brainstorming session. Offer ideas only when it's your turn. Between turns, write down ideas so

TABLE 6.2. Example of Brainstorming

A work group was given the assignment of coming up with a "wish list" for the new company picnic area. Six people got together and generated the following list of ideas:

Wooden picnic tables	Grills
Tables to play checkers on	Soda machine
Patio furniture with umbrellas	Outdoor coolers
Barbecue pit	Fish pond
Relaxing music	Garden walking paths
Snack machine	Water fountain
Multibeverage machine	Exercise stations
Garden compost area	Massage chairs

you don't forget them. Any idea is acceptable, even if it seems silly, strange, or similar to a previous idea. Some of the best ideas are simply variations on what somebody else just said. Say "pass" if you don't have an idea on your turn. Never criticize, question, or even praise others' ideas during the brainstorming session.

At this point, we can also talk about *affinity analysis*, which is just a fancy way of saying look at the list of ideas and see if any of them can be grouped together without losing any of the original intent of the statements. If they can be grouped, then do so by making a summary statement that captures the essence. It is a good idea to get approval from the people who offered the original ideas to make sure nothing is being lost in the combination of ideas. Such analysis has two major advantages: first, it allows for further discussion and refinement of the ideas; second, it reduces the number of items to vote on. In the example in Table 6.2, using affinity analysis may allow us to use the more general term *multibeverage machine* to serve as the essence of two other ideas "soda machine" and "water fountain."

Multivoting

It seems that the average person can't really deal effectively with a list of 20 or 30 items on it. Communication experts tell us that our minds deal with large numbers of items and lists by breaking them into smaller chunks of information. For example, instead of 10 straight numbers to remember, we usually remember our telephone numbers in a series of 3- and 4-number groupings: 888-555-1111. Our Social Security numbers are broken into a 3-2-4 pattern to help us remember: 333-22-4444. And in organizational life, when we get beyond five to seven objectives or goals or ideas, we often get a

TABLE 6.3. Example of Multivoting Results

The work group who brainstormed a wish list for the new company picnic area wanted to narrow down their list of ideas from 16 to 4. Each group member was assigned five votes with which to vote for the topics. Here is the resulting list:

Wooden picnic tables (3)	Grills (6)
Tables to play checkers on (1)	Soda machine (0)
Patio furniture with umbrellas (7)	Outdoor coolers (0)
Barbecue pit (1)	Fish pond (0)
Relaxing music (0)	Garden walking paths (1)
Snack machine (5)	Water fountain (0)
Multibeverage machine (6)	Exercise stations (1)
Garden compost area (0)	Massage chairs (0)

little lost. We have a hard time remembering the 17 key points of the organization, but we can remember better the big three ideas the boss focuses on.

This is where multivoting comes in. Multivoting is a technique used for narrowing a list of ideas or options. It is used in conjunction with brainstorming and is one of several nominal group techniques that help groups work together and make decisions. It is used to make selections based on intensity of viewpoints and majority opinion about certain items of group focus.

The process is relatively straightforward. Use brainstorming to generate a list of topics. Have one person record the ideas on a flip chart. Review and clarify each idea. With the consent of the group, similar ideas can be combined (affinity analysis). Allow each person to have five votes (see Table 6.3 as an example). A vote is something you can use to register your agreement with the item on the list. Giving more than one vote to the same item is a way to measure the intensity of agreement with an item. Have each member assign five votes (or a number that seems reasonable according to the total number of items on the list) to one or more of the ideas (e.g., team members can assign all five votes to one idea, three to one and two to another, one to each of five ideas, or any other combination).

Ask team members to record their points for each idea on a separate note and place the note next to the idea on the flip chart, or have team members call out their votes if the environment is nonthreatening. Another way is to simply have group members come to the flip chart and put a tally mark next to the items they vote for. Tally the votes for each idea. Narrow the list to the four to six ideas that received the most votes. Make sure people feel free to distribute their votes in any way they like. In Table 6.3, we see the results that indicate the four items to be placed in the new picnic area: patio furniture with umbrellas, snack machine, outdoor grills, and a multibeverage machine.

Where Does Voice Fit In?

The first three of the Four Vs are well positioned and highlighted in the STP process. They drive the whole thing. The fourth V, voice, is a bit more subtle. It becomes a group process driver rather than a "box" to fill in. There are three ways voice impacts the STP process: it ensures that everyone is involved, it is a reminder that evaluation is a part of the process, and it becomes a result of the STP process as the organization begins to gain its "voice" through the STP process.

Interaction and input are essential to successful strategic thinking and planning. Only as participants in the process (that is, members of the organization) engage with each other can both comprehensiveness in the decisions and community in implementation be achieved. The concept of voice reminds us that people have choice and that people have skills and interests and creativity that are waiting to be tapped. All of that is essential as we engage in values clarification, vision stories, brainstorming, affinity analysis, and multivoting. Turning *whats* into *hows* also requires *whos*. Voice reminds us of that. A commitment to voice requires us to engage others in the STP process rather than create plans aloof from those who put them into practice.

Plans are also to be evaluated—before, during, and after implementation. Such monitoring of events, after-action reviews, or closure reports need to be built into the STP process. Leaders remember that both they *and* their followers are engaged in the leadership of the organization, and so both are to be involved in the evaluation. Managers alone do not determine the measure of success and do the measuring. The leadership relationship requires many viewpoints and many inputs into evaluations. Such complexity can get cumbersome, and certainly processes need to be in place to manage the system. However, voice reminds us that we need to make the effort to engage multiple perspectives in measuring success and evaluating plans.

The result of thinking and planning together in both strategic and tactical ways is the emergence of a unified voice for the organization. When group members engage together, they begin to share the perspectives, purposes, plans, and principles that guide their work. They begin to speak the same language and see things through the lens of the values, vision, and vectored plans. Perhaps we can call it a culture, but a shared or common organizational voice emerges where group members understand each other better and are better able to explain and exemplify what the organization is all about. Voice, then, is both the underlying commitment in the STP process and the process's result.

Making the Four Vs Real in Action

Ultimately, the Four Vs of Leadership guide us through the STP process and help us organize our work. They also help us simply organize. All too frequently, I see organizations that group themselves by function or by product, rather than by vector. Functional and product oriented organizations are commonplace. In other words, organizations are often organized based on what they do, not why they exist, and so they often forget who they are and begin to do work they should not do or cannot do well. In this way, they change who they are fundamentally and wonder why morale is low, or become confused about how their work links to their values, or they fall into any number of organizational pathologies.

I see this a lot in nonprofit organizations that chase funding streams to "stay alive" but then wonder whether the organization has the kind of life it strove to have in the beginning. As they lose their identity, steeped in values and vision, they engage in work they never intended to do when they started. Often unprepared for such an identity crisis, many of those organizations close up shop. I am not arguing here against innovation, transformation, or organizational flexibility. But often we innovate and transform as a series of incremental opportunistic decisions, rather than through a deliberate process of strategically thinking and planning about ourselves as an organization and as individuals within that organization. So many organizations seem to go with the flow and then complain about where the flow takes them.

Again, some of this is how we chunk up our organizations. The most common ways to establish an organization are by the functional approach, the product approach, and the matrixed approach. They look the way the sound. Functional organizations determine what they do and align themselves accordingly. For example, a business may have marketing, sales, research and development (R&D), and similar functions. Therefore there is a vice president for marketing, one for sales, one for R&D, and so forth. On the other hand, an organization may decide that the focus should be on the products they create. For example, a car company may have subcompact, midsize, luxury, SUV, and hybrid products, hence a vice president for compact car X, one for hybrid car Y, one for SUV Z, and so on. Matrixed organizations combine the wisdom of both functional and product organizations, but at the same time run the risk of having workers

serve two bosses (one functional and one product oriented) with the resultant decline in loyalty and clarity of roles.

The Four Vs, along with the STP process, show us another way to organize: by vectors. Instead of a vice president of sales or a vice president of division X, we would have a vice president of vector 1, whose job it is to ensure
that the strategic goals, objectives, and tasks related to that vector are
achieved and that in the achievement the vector's intent and linkage to
the vision and values remains the same. In this way, accountability is even
clearer in that the actual tasks at hand are the unit of measure, rather than
some generic function or product. The performance measures are not
proxies for success but actually measure the real progress made toward
the real goals.

Using the Four Vs and the related strategic planning model helps link
thinking to planning, leadership to management, people to tasks, tasks to
values, and people to people in collective activities.

The End Results

The end result of the STP process is to link the work of leadership to the
work of getting things done. Leadership is about getting things done. It just
gets things done differently than management does. I recall frequent discussions in training sessions about the need for leadership and the need
for management. Most textbooks reflect the same kind of argument. The
argument goes that both are needed because leaders talk and managers
do. You can't have an organization full of talkers because nothing would
get done. The argument is that no serious thinker would want an organization with only visionaries. There must be some hard-nosed managers
around to get it all done.

And yet there are those who suggest that we should have "leader-full"
organizations. Most leadership development programs state that the goal
is for the managers to do leadership better so that there are leaders at all
levels and all over the organization.

After thinking about leadership and the Four Vs, I have to conclude that
an organization full of leaders is not an organization where people just sit
around, think great thoughts, create vision statements, make speeches,
encourage people through rhetoric, and provide slaps on the back while
nothing ever gets done. No. Rather, an organization full of leaders uses
the Four Vs to inform their thinking, their planning, and their work, and
the thinking, planning, and work of others. Things get done, but without
coercion or a reliance on rank. In management, we manage and change

things; in leadership, we change people's lives, and then *they* change things. Things get done because everyone understands how it all fits together and they have chosen to be stewards of the work, making sure it is all done well so that the organization can thrive within its values and vision framework. The work is done differently, but the jobs get done and done well (perhaps even with genuine enthusiasm).

Points to Ponder

1. Why might it be useful to link strategic thinking to tactical plans? What value, if any, is such a linkage to the worker?
2. How do the values, vision, and vectors boxes clarify the strategic direction and thinking of an organization?
3. How does a strategic thinking foundation clarify the more tactical activities of the organization?
4. What are the relationships between vectors, strategic goals, objectives, actionable items, and action plans?
5. How does measuring performance help an organization's strategic thinking and planning activities?
6. How do the brainstorming, affinity analysis, and multivoting tools work together to help an organization implement the STP process?
7. What does the *what-how* methodology help us accomplish in the STP process?
8. Do you think it is possible (and advantageous) to have an organization full of leaders? Why or why not?

Quotables

1. "Effective leadership is putting first things first. Effective management is discipline, carrying it out." —Stephen Covey, author and businessman
2. "In God we trust, all others bring data." —Edward Deming, American statistician and management consultant
3. "That business purpose and business mission are so rarely given adequate thought is perhaps the most important cause of business frustration and failure." —Peter Drucker, management consultant and author

Practical Activities

1. *Working the Process.* The best way to understand how the Four Vs help organizations think and plan strategically is to try them out a few times. Pick a group you are familiar with (at work, civic group, church group, family, or other). Work through the STP process from values to action plans. Make

note of what works for you and what needs improvement. Then try it out again with another group.

2. *A Vector Organization.* Think of an organization you know well. Or create a hypothetical organization. Draw its current organization chart and determine whether it is a functional, product-oriented, or matrixed organization. Then determine the organization's current or potential vectors with associate goals, objectives and action plans. With the vectors outlined, draw an organization chart using the vectors as the unit of divisions within the organization. Add to the chart the areas of stewardship (goals, objectives, and action plans) the leader of each vector section would have. Compare and contrast the current organization chart with the vector organization chart. Determine what benefits might accrue from organizing around vectors. Determine what steps might be needed to move from the current organization chart to one based on vectors.

Chapter 7

Four Vs, Four 'Ems of Management, and Five Perspectives of Leadership

The Four Vs of leadership framework helps us both describe leadership and put leadership into action. In so doing, it also distinguishes the technologies of leadership from those of management. In this chapter, we will discuss this distinction more fully. In so doing, we will also see that what some people may view as leadership really is grounded much more in the notions of management. We will see that some values and some sources of power tend us toward leadership, and some tend us toward management with correspondingly serious consequences for how people interact and how organizations both function generally and view their members specifically.

Management Root

To begin this discussion, I turn to the root meanings of the terms *management* and *leadership*; and while the study of word roots is not an exact science, I commend the printed and online etymology dictionaries for help in this effort. We will turn our attention first to management roots.

Imagine a scene in sixteenth-century France where knights in shining armor galloped across the land on their trusty steeds. For this grand scene to make sense, we have to have, of course, a trusty steed. Hence, the need to tame horses, and train them well, was a reality of the times. Some of the knights' faithful servants became very good horse tamers. They quickly learned that their main goal was to break the horse's spirit, to break its will in such a way that, over time, the animal completely submitted to the knight's desires. So how do we break a horse's spirit? How do you divest the horse of its will? I claim no real expertise in that, but apparently, one must do things like ride the horse until it tires and no longer resists. A less gentle tamer may employ a whip or tight ropes or even lay a hand on the animal in forceful ways. The goal, ultimately, is complete submission to the knight's will, with no concern for the horse's will at all—a will that hopefully has been beaten out of it.

Breaking a horse makes sense because what knight in his right mind would want to ride into battle atop a creative or willful horse? Rather, the knight needs the horse to do exactly what the knight wants it to do, when he wants it to do it, the way he wants it to do it, every time. As arrows fly and swords are unsheathed, we don't want the horse to start thinking what would be best. Rather, the knight wants the horse to perform the way the knight wants and needs it to. Riding a creative, willful horse into battle is not ideal. Or when the damsel is in distress and the knight rides off to save her, he doesn't really want the horse to suggest multiple courses of action or to hesitate because it deems the damsel less than worthy of its efforts. The horse helps the knight fulfill the *knight's* will and desires and achieve the knight's goals. The horse's will, desires, and goals are irrelevant. The fewer deviations from the knight's will and the better the horse obeys its master, the better the trusty steed is in the eyes of the knight.

Sixteenth-century horsemen in France developed a word to describe how they handled and tamed horses. This word was *manège*, which most likely comes from the Italian, *maneggiare*, which comes from the Latin root for "hand," from which we also get the phrase *mano a mano*, or "hand to hand." The French adopted this term to describe how they put hand to horse to control it. The sense is that complete submission was achievable as a rider handled (put hand to) the horse. From this evolved our current English verb "to manage" and a little later the overall notion of "management."

In essence, the root of the word is still the foundation of the concept: management means "beating a horse into submission." Perhaps that is a bit strong, but management is about the seeking of submission and control of others to accomplish what the manager wants (regardless, we might add, of the desires of the "horse"). Management is about control, obedience, and routine to achieve predictable behavior over time that conforms to standards that can be measured and made more efficient.

Management relies on making decisions and then finding people to carry them out in controlled, predictable, consistent, and measurable ways so that improvement can be made over time. There is no necessary need for concern about the people doing the work. In fact, much effort is made in pure management theory to turn the people into mere cogs in the machine. The less we have to deal with the fickleness of people, the better. The less we have to deal with emotional outbursts, or bad days, or poor attitudes, the more efficiently the work can be accomplished. When we don't have to worry about the spirit and will of others doing the work, we can focus more on the work and efficiency improvements. You get the idea. Management as an organizational concept and technology tries hard to take the "people stuff" out of the work.

We even have new terms for workers. We give them job series numbers and refer to them as position descriptions rather than as people. I was a federal government "301 Administration Generalist" for a while myself. Better yet, we sometimes call workers FTEs—full-time equivalents. This means that the person is referred to merely as a job filler that works the equivalent of 40 hours a week.

Management works on things; we manage things, and when we try to manage people, we need to turn them into things—without wills or spirits of their own. FTEs are things rather than people. The beautiful thing about FTEs is that we can do things to them we would never do to people. We may be more inclined to yell at FTEs, to ignore an FTE's plea to be home for his child's birthday party that evening rather than stay late to finish a report, or to dismiss an FTE's suggestion. It is a common practice in budget cutting or reductions in force to downgrade a function to less time or to reduce staff by some fraction of an FTE allocation. In other words we cut FTEs in half, which is something we wouldn't do to people. We reduce FTEs or divide them into fractional FTEs without worrying about any impact on people. We can even require that FTEs be moved around the country in consolidation efforts without any concern for a person's mortgage, or children, or the like.

Indeed, management prefers "things," because "people" inject too many variables of potential inefficiencies and too many distractions. Perhaps the most common reminder of this depersonalization is what we often call people who are lower than management in the hierarchy—subordinates. This word comes from the Latin prefix *sub*, meaning "under" or "below," and the root *ordinare*, which means "to arrange," or "to count," or "to make intervals." Together the word *subordinate* means "someone who is not worthy of being counted." And that is what management depends upon—people who are not counted as people but rather as things to be controlled to achieve predictable behavior over time.

Leadership Root

Leadership has very different roots. Around the same time as our French friends were taming horses, their English counterparts were sailing ships, using their expertise in navigation. To find their own way and chart their own courses, these mariners depended on what they called the *lodestar* (more commonly known today as the North Star or Polaris). They relied on the lodestar because of its consistency of nature and its profound potential influence in the night skies because of that consistency. It was a relatively bright star. It was always where it should be. It didn't move much and so was reliable. It had, in a sense, an integrity to it. By relying on the lodestar, a ship's captain could determine where he was and where he needed to go, and make his own choices as to how best to get to the destination. He was able to know where to go, because he knew where he was, ever-guided as to how to get there. He could do all of this without the lodestar ever laying a hand on him or saying a word. Its influence and its integrity were enough.

The term *lodestar* is significant because its roots are shared with the more modern term *lead*. Lodestar comes from the Old English word *lædan*, which means basically "to cause to go with one" or "to guide," having emerged from Old Norse or Germanic terms (such as *liden*, *lithan*, *leith*, *or laithjan*) that have to do with traveling, going on a journey, or "to go in a way." A related word is the Old English *lad*, which means "way, course, carrying." Attach these meanings to the star that guides and carries travelers on their own journeys, and we get the lodestar. From these terms emerged the word *lead* and *leader*, with the general concept of *leadership* emerging toward the beginning of the nineteenth century.

These roots laid a foundation that describes leadership in terms of guidance, direction, consistency, and journeying together toward perhaps mutually agreed upon directions. It is not about control; it is not about the leader's wishes, per se. Leadership is about leader and follower working together from a common vantage point, while encouraging freedom of choice and actions, to accomplish what leader and led can both agree is beneficial, with a heavy emphasis on the follower's will, spirit, and capacities.

The bottom line is that there is a strong element of collaboration in a cause or on a journey in the ideas of leadership; conversely, there is a strong element of control in the ideas of management.

The Four 'Ems of Management

As the Four Vs described in this book help us understand the nature and practice of leadership, we can compare with great benefit some practical activities of management to our overall understanding of both concepts. So here I introduce the Four *'Ems* of Management as a pithy way to express ways we try to control others so that predictable behavior results. We will see that the activities of management and those of leadership have little resemblance because the philosophy and intended results of both have very little in common.

Here Are the Four 'Ems: Walk 'Em, Sock 'Em, Talk 'Em, and Mock 'Em

The goals of the Four 'Ems are the goals of management: to develop subordinates who have controlled and predictable behavior over time consistent with the management's wishes and decisions. The four techniques are employed specifically when a subordinate starts to inject his or her own will, personality, or humanness into the picture, but they are also used to maintain control and keep an eye on things generally.

The first is Walk 'em. This means to fire people who aren't controllable, trainable, or predictable. It can also mean transferring them to someone else, giving another division the "problem children" instead of dealing with them yourself. Because management as an organizational technology does not depend on the consideration of other people's feelings, values, or general contributions, and because people's overall life situation is of little consequence in the transactional arrangement which is work, if workers can't handle it, then management can and will fire them. And managers should, if they want the goals of management to be fulfilled. Once management removes the problem employees, management simply hires new people with similar skills and begins to train them into behaving predictably within the management scheme of the organization.

An imperfect example may help illustrate the point. Imagine an underperforming second baseman on a professional baseball team. After trying for a while to fit him into the system, the team's manager simply releases the second baseman and hires a new one with similar skills. One second baseman is like another second baseman, each with similar skills and understanding of the game. But if one can behave predictably within the parameters of the management of the team, that second baseman stays. This benefits the second baseman and the team as a whole. An underperforming player, who can't get with the system and who clashes with the management, would not be counted a "trusty steed," as we might put it. Such players will not be asked to go into battle with the rest of the team; they will be asked to take a hike, to take a walk away from the organization. They will be asked to leave; they will be fired.

Of course, this 'Em has consequences. It is disruptive to fire people. Because people are people and not merely subordinates, there will be some formal and informal discussions about the firing, especially from those who remain. Some may fear for their own jobs, and productivity may be negatively impacted, in the short term at least. It can be hurtful to an organization. However, it can also be helpful. Often, workers are just waiting and hoping the boss will finally get rid of "that guy." The action can reiterate for others what the standards are and what conformance to those standards looks like. For some workers, firing a less-than-productive employee may serve as a needed and appreciated reminder of what work is expected and how it is to be done.

Certainly, walking 'em can be helpful. My hope, though, is that it never becomes fun for the manager who does it. I can imagine bosses who relish the chance to fire people. Rather than losing any sleep, some managers enjoy the exercise of power over others. This reveling in power is a warning flag for the functions of management. Controlling others may be necessary in managerial terms, but when the management looks forward to exercising power over others, it is just wrong.

A young, executive officer faced this dilemma at a university campus business fraternity. The fraternity was suffering from a high inactivity rate among its more senior members, which caused the group to suffer in terms of national recognitions and awards. The executive committee began a concerted effort to reclaim these inactive members. Interestingly, one of the first proposals was to expel them. The sentiment expressed is that when they were initiated into the fraternity, attendance was a requirement that they took an oath to fulfill. Many people, the officers believed, were not living up to their promises. By policy, expulsion is a potential result of not attending enough meetings, and the executive committee thought it should punish them accordingly.

However, as the officer explained it, she realized this approach would defeat the purpose of trying to bring members back. She continued to rationalize this punishment of expulsion, though, making it easier for her to swallow this kind of tough medicine. She said things like, "This would show the new members that we mean business and we are not an organization that a person can just throw on their resume"; or "This act of discipline would show the current members that inactivity is not accepted and give them more of an incentive to stay active." The idea was that while punishing a few, the existing members and the new crop of members would get the message and start attending. This is the value of walking 'em, and management does it a lot.

The story is interesting, too, because of what the officer began to think about. For her it brought up an important question of whether or not a leader can punish a follower. She recognized that, currently, the executive team was acting as managers who run the organization. To switch over from managers to leaders they would need to develop a values set with the members. The officer realized that using authority to punish could damage the shared values and make the members look at the executives more as people of authority rather than people who want to be there to lead and mentor them. True, indeed. Leaders lead followers, but managers deal with subordinates, workers, employees, and numbers. The question of punishment, the nature of it, and the relationship and status of both the giver and receiver is a question relevant to the next technique as well.

The second practice is Sock 'em. This means to punish a subordinate for improper, substandard work (not doing it the way the manager wants it or management standards demand it be done), inappropriate attitudes, or expressions of personal will (not behaving the way management prescribes). There are formal and there are informal punishments. We can put subordinates "on report." We can dock their pay or suspend their employment. We can give a poor performance rating that impacts future pay or promotions. We can as easily take them "behind the woodshed" and give them a stern reminder of proper behavior and attitude. Or we can take away a privilege they had previously enjoyed. There are many ways of punishing workers to encourage conformance to managerial norms and standards, perhaps restricted only to the imagination of the boss and the limits of the law.

However, like with the Walk 'em technique, there are consequences. Some of the coworkers might be relieved or excited that so-and-so is finally getting what is due. People know who is slacking at the office, and they are often grateful that the boss finally has the courage or wherewithal to do something about it. Yet there may be some coworkers who would fear for their position in the office or worry that some benefit may be withheld from them or some punishment administered. For management, the key consideration is that by socking 'em, they will retain or enhance the controlled and predictable behavior over time that they wish for. If, as a result, more Sock 'ems are needed to get other employees to conform, so be it.

The third technique to control and manage others may be the most popular and perhaps may be considered the nicest. The goal is still to help others know and conform to management's depiction of the work to be done in the best possible way. This technique is Talk 'em. When management decides to talk with a subordinate about low or nonstandard performance, the intent is to diagnose the problem and eliminate it. Less formally, this occurs through unilateral feedback, where the boss sees something nonconforming in the behavior of the worker and points it out in a way that intends to get the worker back on track.

I use the term *unilateral feedback* because in a management mode, there is very little desire or need to hear from the worker. The issue is seen as management needing to tell the worker how better to conform to management guidelines, work procedures, or the like. One-way communication that intends to control the behavior of the worker to be more controlled and predictable is what this feedback is all about.

You can contrast this feedback with a multilateral feedback approach where the intent is not conformity, per se, but unity around the cause. The goal is understanding and the development of trust around core values that elicits better work that will move the cause forward in positive ways. Multilateral feedback suggests that the worker has something to offer the work plans and decisions, and that the leader would be willing and excited to hear and even include the ideas into the organizational goals and plans. Such multilateral feedback requires an admission that workers are people with skills, values, ideas, freedom, and so on that would be helpful to the work, even if it changes some of the current norms. It is not a control technique but a developmental and improvement technique.

But the Talk 'em process is really a unilateral process. Even the more formal Talk 'em approaches are really unilateral in nature. These more formal approaches take the form of scheduled meetings and structured discussions with workers. For instance, a worker shows up for work late 8 out of the last 10 days. The boss has been patient up to now, giving only a few informal feedbacks the last two weeks. But now it is time to get this problem resolved. The boss calls the worker into the office. Across a desk from each other, the boss begins by stating the problem and asking for reasons why the worker has been late and even soliciting ideas as to why the worker shouldn't be punished. Performance evaluations and individual development plans are brought up. Perhaps they decide on some training the worker should receive or, if needed, the boss refers the worker to an employee assistance program to deal with personal issues (which of course the boss has no desire or time to deal with). The hope is that some of these plans will get the worker to conform by coming to work on time, by not disrupting the work flow because of the tardiness, and by being productive like everyone else. Of course, if the worker doesn't comply, there is always Walk 'em and Sock 'em to fall back on.

The Talk 'em technique does require the boss to be an amateur psychologist, but only up to a point. It requires the boss to be willing to devote time to more formal meetings and improvement plans. It requires management to devote resources to the training, retraining, and counseling of workers. On the face of it, Talk 'em is an ethical, even nice, approach—certainly less drastic than the previous two.

Some managers find Talk 'em a fun and useful way to get the work accomplished in a more efficient and predictable manner. But not every manager is up to the task. Not every boss does it well. Setting aside the hurt or help this approach may have on the manager or the other workers who witness the attempts, some bosses are just uncomfortable confronting workers in a sincere desire to get them to shape up. Perhaps it is easier just to fire them or transfer them to another division. Done poorly, talking to workers and having formal meetings and plans may even increase the formal grievances workers make against their bosses, thus gumming up productivity even more. Certainly, Talk 'em has its ups and its downs, but it is still designed to gain controlled, predictable behavior over time.

The technique that does not have any ups, only downs in my opinion, is Mock 'em. To mock workers is to marginalize them in such a way that they don't matter anymore in the organization, that what they say is unimportant, that what they do is immaterial. Mocking either forces them to conform to avoid the mocking or to quit by their own choice, thus avoiding paperwork and management focus away from the "real work" of the office. Both outcomes are desirable to a management that employs the technique. So how do we mock others at work? I am reluctant to say it, but I believe this technique is used more often than we think. A few examples may show how subtle and pervasive it is.

I remember the story of a woman who worked at a company that makes and sells signs all over the country. One of her jobs was to develop a script to use on the phone during sales calls. After working hard on the project, she presented it to her boss. The boss immediately rejected it and wrote his own script to be used. This result is not uncommon. I myself experienced similar management actions when upper management summarily dismissed a process-reengineering effort without taking the time to figure out what my team had done and why. These kinds of actions by managers serve to belittle the efforts of people. The rejection of honest and diligent work without acknowledgment of any effort is a form of mocking others, of discounting them as people who are capable and committed.

There is another story about a gymnastics coach who seemed to have favorites. Her assistant coach saw this immediately. The coach motivated the gymnasts that she favored and expressed a common courtesy toward them; however, if she did not favor a gymnast, she would openly make a joke about him or her. The coach would focus on improving only the gymnasts with ability or the gymnasts that she favored. Such a decision by someone in authority is another example of how easy it is to Mock 'em, and, frankly, how often we sometimes do it.

Consider also what it is to "dress down" employees in public, or in other words, to yell at them for poor performance or a mistake made. It happens often. The consequence is that the workers feel put upon. They feel mistreated. They feel ignored. They feel the boss doesn't care. All of these things make people feel less like people of equal value and more like people who aren't worthy of being counted. Remember that woman at the sign company. She finally decided to quit (this is mocking 'em morphing into walking 'em). As she walked down the hall, saying goodbye to friends and coworkers, she ran into the boss. She said that instead of questioning her on how things were going, if she had found new work or interested businesses, or if she needed something to help the transition, the boss simply asked, "You're still here?" This was the last straw to the employee. She felt as though she was nothing in the eyes of the man who was her supervisor. It is hard to find a better summary of the results of mocking.

There is an effect on those in the office who witness the mocking of coworkers or hear about it later. Often, they react in support of the boss, and little by little coworkers begin to dismiss the mocked employee as well. The coworkers listen to the targeted employee less; they go to him or her less for help or guidance. Others realize that the targeted person is on the boss's bad list and so they associate with the person less. Little by little, that worker is marginalized, mattering less and less in terms of the work being done. When we disparage others, talk down to them, or talk bad about them, we are mocking 'em. Another way to Mock 'em is to build an "organizational shelf" and then place the worker on it, thus isolating them from the work being done and from the other workers. The shelf is metaphorical, of course, but it is a way of making people unimportant to the work being done and therefore unable to cause disruptions in the overall work generally and the behaviors of other workers specifically.

A story about such shelf building is illustrated by the experience of one young bureaucrat in a federal cabinet agency. The boss had identified a poor performer who was disrupting the work and other workers. The boss's diagnosis was that the employee was talking too much to others in the office and distracting them from the work, not fulfilling the main responsibilities he had been hired to do, and that he had, basically, outlived his usefulness. Tough things to hear. But this young management assistant heard them because the boss told him to "fix the problem."

As the management assistant began to work on the problem (never once talking directly to the employee in question or making a distinction between issues of concern and the person involved), he realized there were some duties the office needed to fulfill but hadn't in the recent past. These duties mainly involved representing the organization at national and regional conferences that occurred fairly regularly all year long. To make a long story short, the management assistant took this problem employee who had the ability to talk a lot, who was experienced enough to represent the organization, and who the boss didn't want in the office to disrupt the work flow, and created a shelf for him.

The shelf consisted of the employee traveling to all of these conferences and meetings and upon his return writing a short memo summarizing the trip. An office need left unfulfilled before was now being done, and the employee was never in the office because he was always on the road. In fact, he was out of the office so much that newer employees didn't even know who he was and soon, he was forgotten. Even the summary memos, frankly, were not missed if they failed to arrive on the boss's desk.

At the time, the management assistant felt he was doing good service to both the office and the worker. The employee still had a job, the boss was happy he wasn't around, and the office even got something done they hadn't been able to do before. But looking back, the management assistant realized how he had treated this person and the effect it had on the employee in terms of the work. The management assistant had defined the employee as a problem, not a person. The assistant created an environment where the employee was unimportant in the office. Management conspired to make the work the employee did immaterial to the real stuff of the organization. The employee was marginalized and forgotten. The management assistant mocked him into being irrelevant. Over time, this management assistant no longer patted himself on the back about solving this problem as he recognized the control techniques he used. From this story we can learn that people are people not problems or things to be fixed. However, conquering a history or culture of mocking others is difficult. And I have a feeling mocking still happens in organizations all the time.

The effect of all these efforts to mock and marginalize is predictable. Often, that person who has been acted upon conforms and works harder, keeps his head down, contributes only what is needed the way it was told to be done and nothing more, becomes docile, and submits to the will of management. Or he doesn't. If the worker doesn't begin to conform, either he stays employed but has no real input or impact in any way and is ignored totally by the organization, or he leaves, either on his own or because management walks 'em. Either way, management gets what it wants: controlled, predictable behavior out of workers without the headaches. Is this an ethical approach? It happens a lot more often than we give ourselves credit for, but popularity isn't a criterion for ethical behavior.

Influence and "Power With"

If control and power over people are the hallmark of the Four 'Ems of Management, then influence and a focus on "power with" other people (as opposed to "power over" others) is more in line with leadership. When we describe leadership (as distinct from management) and its corresponding techniques, the purposes of teaching and refining values, and the impact of principles on how we are and how we do things, we touch on that very important element of leadership based on relationship called *influence*. Chapter 1 reminds us that power and influence are linked in that influence is measured by the resultant change in behavior, values, efforts, ideas, and actions of some actual use of power emanating from a particular source of power. Certainly, influential people lead. They guide; they motivate; they inspire. But they never force.

To influence is literally to cause an inward flowing that impacts the nature, character, or destiny of the object in question. We influence others when we cause to flow into them a certain way of being, doing, believing, or seeing. The degree to which we impact such things is a measure of our influence or power, whether great or small. In a very real sense, we influence others as we engage in tactics that elicit some degree of change. These tactics are grounded in some sense of power that we can tap into.

Two social psychologists in the 1950s, John French and Bertram Raven, suggested that we can tap into five sources of power: coercive power, reward power, legitimate power, expert power, and referent power.[1] Although some have critiqued their research, these five sources of power have the virtues of being easy to understand and broad in coverage of the ideas of power. Another well-known leadership author, Stephen Covey, suggests there are only three real types or sources of power: coercive power, utility power, and principle-centered power. Others divide power into only positional power or personal power. However we parse the idea of power, it is still the capacity to influence other people, and that capacity is gained from different sources.

I often simplify the matter by suggesting that there are two types of power that encapsulate not only the different sources of power but also the intent of the use of that power as well: power over others, and power with others. In previous chapters we discussed the ideas of acting and being acted upon. Here, we see that power *over* others is linked to acting upon others, while power *with* others is linked to acting for ourselves and encouraging others to act.

If we further distinguish leadership from management, leadership is about acting and allowing others to act and hence must use power-with techniques and sources, while management is about acting upon others and uses power-over techniques and sources.

To be clearer on these generic sources of power, each is summarized and depicted on a continuum of power found in Figure 7.1. Coercive power involves the extent to which a person can deny desired rewards or administer punishment to control other people. These rewards and punishments can be physical, symbolic, or emotional in nature, and the efficacy of coercive power is reactive and temporary, depending on the fear of the followers. Reward power revolves around how a person can use extrinsic or intrinsic rewards to control people. Accessing and using these rewards depends on a person's skill and resources.

FIGURE 7.1. Sources of Power

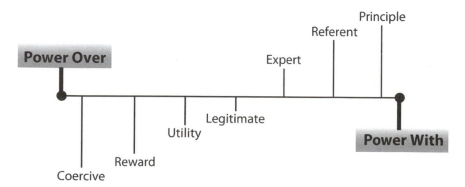

Utility power involves influencing others based on an exchange of valued things. The exercise of this power causes people to follow because of the benefit that comes to them if they do. It is temporary in nature and depends on both how well one discerns the things of value and how people view the fairness and equity of the exchanges. Legitimate power, or formal hierarchical authority, is about how much people believe that the boss has a "right" to dictate action or command and control behavior. Of course, if the belief about that right to direct others changes, so does the legitimacy (and usefulness) of that power.

Expert power gets its capacity to influence another person by possessing knowledge, experience, or judgment that is perceived by others to be greater than their own. It is a personal power source and is by definition relative, depending on one's level of "expertise" and on others' perceptions of that expertise.

Referent power is another personal power source. This power source involves someone influencing another based on the other person's desire to identify with the power source. For example, a person wants to be like the person of power and hence wants to do what the person does, look how the person looks, and know and socialize with the same kinds of people.

If we add to referent power the ideas of morality and vision, we begin to see what principle power is all about. In principle power, not only does a person want to be like or do like the power source, the person is also influenced because she believes in the leader and what he or she stands for. Who the leader is, not just what he or she does or who he or she knows, is the source of power. Hence, this source elicits trust, respect, commitment, and a sense of honor and consistency.

This source of power is sustainable over long periods of time and is a proactive influence based on values of the parties involved. If control is evident at all in the interaction, it is a self-control chosen and exerted by leader and follower grounded in mutually held values and morality.

For me, a key question in leadership is: from what source of power do I ground my influence tactics and leadership approaches? Answering this question does beg the questions: "Is leadership different based on different sources of power?" and "Do some sources of power tend toward management, others toward leadership, and still others toward something else, like oppression and tyranny?" These questions inevitably link to notions of values as well. Do some values cause us to prefer some power sources over others? Can we determine the type of power used by determining the values people hold? Can such a determination tell us something of their leadership? Of their management?

Evaluating Other People's Leadership: Perspectives of Leadership and the Four Vs

These questions lead us to a discussion of how we can use the Four Vs to evaluate other people's leadership. The Four Vs outline techniques and even mind-sets about leadership that we can adopt and apply. But the framework also provides a way to describe and analyze the leadership we see in others. All of us have our opinions about leadership, and few of those opinions are in much agreement. In other words, people see things differently sometimes, and leadership is no exception.

In fact, elsewhere I have written about different perspectives of leadership that people may hold. There are at least five (see Figure 7.2). Although these perspectives may or may not be objectively true, people act as if they are true for them, and it impacts how they view the activities of their own leadership and the way they measure and make decisions about the leadership of others. Each perspective is unique, and adherents to one are not adherents to another, at least not unless they are moving from one to another. The five perspectives include the following:

1. People who believe leadership is simply management and based on position and rank (leadership as management)
2. People who believe leadership is about using position and rank to constantly improve toward excellence the worker, the work flow, and the workplace (leadership as excellence management)
3. People who believe leadership is about getting others to believe in a values set that is compelling for the work or cause at hand and acting according to those values (values leadership)

FIGURE 7.2. The Five Perspectives of Leadership

4. People who believe leadership is about making trust and cultures of trust the most important value upon which to build shared governance and community (trust culture leadership)
5. People who believe leadership is an activity based on core values that make people whole people, the goal of which is to liberate the best in people, to ennoble each other in the work we decide to do together (whole-soul or spiritual leadership)

Each of these perspectives differs in descriptions, tools, behaviors, and approaches to followers. But we can also see that the Four Vs are a way of detecting the descriptions, tools, behaviors, and approaches of followers. In that sense, using the principles and ideas of the Four Vs of leadership, we can determine which perspective is at play and which is not. We can even determine whether leadership is at play at all. It is another way that the Four Vs framework can be used to describe, diagnose, and determine leadership behavior.

Each of these perspectives has implicit assumptions about the kinds of power used and the types of values that guide leadership activities. Each perspective has its own underlying assumptions (values, vision, vectors, and commitment to voice) that can be analyzed.

For instance, leadership as management relies heavily on positional power to guide its efforts, and the values of efficiency and productivity would be much more likely to ground behavior than values like fairness or trust. Not that fairness and trust don't enter into the equation, but the main variables have more to do with managerial conformance, and hence the values tend toward obedience, discipline, and efficiency. Contrast that with what seems implicit in whole-soul leadership, which is more in line with valuing free will, human flourishing, self-confidence, selflessness, and similar values. We begin to see that there are stark differences in the power sources and values at play among these five perspectives.

The Four Vs of Leadership are still relevant in each perspective, but the Vs have a qualitatively different feel from one perspective to another. The values, vision, vectors, and respect for voice in each perspective differ from one another. And so we see that the Four Vs are a very useful way of figuring out just what kind of leadership is going on and whether the leadership is leadership at all. An example may be helpful.

The example is a stark one. We'll discuss whether or not Hitler was a leader. I bring this up because it frequently comes up in leadership courses I have conducted. I often ask participants to think of leaders, living or dead, and I make a list of them. It is surprising the similarities of those lists I have observed over the years. Names of presidents, CEOs, philanthropists, clergy, athletes, and so on make the list. Part of the goal of this exercise is to have the participants become familiar with each other and feel comfortable throwing out ideas. It begins the process of dissecting what they assume leadership to be.

Inevitably, participants achieve these goals. People become comfortable enough to be provocative (which of course means that good discussions are not far behind). And so, over time, the list begins to include people like Hitler, Pol Pot of the Khmer Rouge, and Genghis Khan alongside the initial names of Washington, Gandhi, Mother Teresa, Martin Luther King Jr., Lincoln, and so on. These lists always interest me.

In fact, I confess these kinds of lists got me interested in leadership a long time ago. I was curious about how those lists could come about. How can a discussion defining *leaders* include so many different types of people, even people who on the face of it are so disparate in their beliefs, behaviors, and impacts? To hear that a leader is someone like Gandhi and Hitler, Pol Pot and Mother Teresa, Julius Caesar and Jesus Christ, Genghis Khan and George Washington is very odd to me. How can people with such varying and divergent values sets all be considered (at least by some) leaders? I wondered if leadership was all things to all people and therefore nothing really.

Frankly, I was uncomfortable accepting that the above lists were true. I wanted to believe that some of those people were leaders and some of them just weren't. It turns out that combining the Four Vs of Leadership framework with the idea of leadership perspectives provides a sound analysis tool that suggests what I wanted to believe about leadership was actually true.

Back to the list. Inevitably, someone is brave enough to yell out, "How about Hitler? He was a leader." I ask the others whether they agree, and they always do. Yes, Hitler is a leader. Then I ask them if Hitler is their leader. To date, no one has said yes. How can it be, I ask, that Hitler is a leader, but he isn't *your* leader? The answer: we don't believe what he believed in. But then someone says, "Yeah, but some people did and still do." So right away, we intuitively know that values play a key role in understanding leadership and that voice is an implicit necessity in the leadership relationship. Some chose to follow Hitler and some didn't. What is that choice based on? We know now it is based on the values, vision, vectors, and the relative respect to voice that Hitler articulated or embodied.

I think we can see that Hitler followed the Four Vs framework. He had values, and a vision that flowed from them, with vectors that accomplished his vision. We accept, though, that sometimes his comfort with voice in the leadership relationship was suspect. Indeed, some did choose to believe and were *able* to choose. But many others in his sphere of growing influence didn't have a real choice because of coercive tactics or a climate of fear and harsh treatment. In this sense, Hitler's leadership may not have been leadership to the degree that he diminished the free choice given to followers to follow. So at best, Hitler was a values-based leader. Trust and a commitment to ennobling values were not on the top of his list, as the results of his actions can attest.

However, he certainly did articulate a set of values and provide vision and direction. He chose a set of values out of the many possible and shaped a vision and vectors from it. In the values leadership perspective, leadership does not depend on any sense of normatively good values, just on values that trigger behavior, and all of them do. His values set was different from what the participants in the training group would suggest are worthy of following; therefore they don't view him as their leader. However, some in Hitler's day did find value in following him, and they did follow. To those who subscribe to values leadership, Hitler was indeed a leader and did the things of leadership. The only caveat may be the degree to which he respected and allowed for voice to play a role in his endeavors.

However, to a person who feels that leadership is a whole-soul or spiritual endeavor, there is more analysis to do. They may ask the values leader, "Is that all we ask of leadership? Is it merely to cobble together some values upon which to lead, or is there some moral goodness, some direction to our values, some ennobling requirement to leadership?" In the values leadership perspective, there really isn't. But in the whole-soul or spiritual leadership perspective, there certainly is. Leadership is based on core values of humanity, the best in all of us. The intent of leadership is to change people's lives for the better, not just to change them. There is a moral and normative direction to our activities of leadership. In that sense, then, Hitler misses the mark. He is no leader in that perspective.

This example of analyzing "leadership" teaches us that using the Four Vs of Leadership framework, along with the identified leadership perspectives, we can be much more sophisticated in our leadership analyses. Is Hitler a leader? Hitler is a leader, sure. But he isn't a leader to the degree that he limits voice, and he certainly is a leader only under the values leadership perspective at best. Is Hitler a leader? No way, not if we believe leadership is a whole-soul, spiritual endeavor helping us be the best we can be in an ennobling and moral effort to progress. Is Hitler a leader? Final answer: yes, sort of, but not to me and not for the improvement of the human soul. So my intellectual curiosity is resolved, at least a little. Hitler isn't a leader to me. He may not even be a leader at all. And that just feels right to me. I may take him off the list.

To be more general, though, we can see that there are certain values and visions that tend themselves toward different leadership perspectives. So it matters what values and sources of power you choose to engage with as you choose to lead others. Some values will make you a manager at best. Some will make you a leader. And some will simply make you a power wielder.

Clarifying to yourself what perspective of leadership you hold in combination with the values you feel are important in the work you do with others is therefore a worthy endeavor. It is something all who engage in leadership do, whether they know it or not. The concepts laid out thus far give us a chance to make these ideas explicit to ourselves so that we do leadership just that much more intentionally.

Points to Ponder

1. How do the roots of the words *management* and *leadership* help us understand the technology of management and leadership?
2. What impact on people and organizations is there as we treat people as "things" in our efforts to manage?
3. How can you be a "lodestar" in the organizations to which you belong?
4. How do the Four 'Ems of Management reinforce management's focus on control? Which 'Em seems to be the most used in the organizations with which you have experience?
5. With which sources of power do you feel most comfortable?
6. How do the ideas of "power over" and "power with" help you understand leadership and management?
7. With which of the five perspectives of leadership do you most associate? Do you feel a need to explore any other perspectives?
8. What do you think about the idea that some people may consider someone a leader who may not be a leader to you? How do the five perspectives change the way you define and analyze leaders both living and dead?

Quotables

1. "Management is about arranging and telling. Leadership is about nurturing and enhancing." —Tom Peters, author
2. "If a rhinoceros were to enter this restaurant now, there is no denying he would have great power here. But I should be the first to rise and assure him that he had no authority whatever." —G. K. Chesterton, author

3. "Great leaders are almost always great simplifiers, who can cut through argument, debate, and doubt to offer a solution everybody can understand." — General Colin Powell

Practical Activities

1. *Real-Time Observation.* Choose someone you know who you consider to be a leader. Observe him or her in the leadership role for at least a month. In your observations, keep track of the values and vision this person expresses. How are they expressed? Determine whether the vectors, if there are any, are aligned with values and vision. Discern the sources of power this person relies on. Are those sources of power in line with the values and vision he or she expresses? Are multiple sources of power used? Can you observe a preferred source of power? Ultimately, determine which of the five perspectives of leadership this leader may adopt as his or her own. Is that the perspective of leadership you have?

2. *Five Perspectives and Values.* Make a list of personal and organizational values that are commonly presented as important, for example, efficiency, integrity, customer service, kindness, compassion, dependability, innovation, etc. Then place those values within the perspective of leadership you think is most relevant or most conducive to the fulfillment of or is the embodiment of that value. Determine your leadership perspective by figuring out which values you currently feel are important at work. Then determine which values you wish were currently valued at work. Is there a difference? Do you sense a need to change your perspective of leadership accordingly?

Note

1. John French and Bertram Raven, "The Bases of Social Power," in *Studies of Social Power*, ed. Dorwin Cartwright (Ann Arbor, MI: Institute for Social Research, 1959).

Chapter 8

Conclusion

Clearing up your values and helping others see the value of personal and organizational values is the beginning of leadership. Values and principles wrapped in the fundamental notion of free will and choice, and energized by meaning, purposeful activity, and direction are the foundation of all leadership activities. These are the things that make people choose to follow. If any of these elements are violated, diminished, or restricted, then the leadership itself is diminished to that degree.

If we restrict voice and rely more on rank and position to impact other people, then leadership is really not much more than management. The first two perspectives, leadership as management and leadership as excellence management, described in chapter 7, show us this. The last three perspectives (values leadership, trust culture leadership, and whole-soul/spiritual leadership) teach us that having a values foundation, perhaps even focusing on trust and the core values of humanity, is the essence of leadership. It is only when we recognize the power of principles, the value of volition, and the inspiration of purpose and direction do we act in ways that reveal real leadership.

For this reason, if I wanted to increase my leadership, I would make my values more explicit in my own life and in my interactions and discussions with others. I would have to choose some values over others. I would have to accept that some values have certain consequences and results that I do not like, which I should avoid as I interact with others. I would also have to accept that I am comfortable with other values and their corresponding consequences and that those principles make sense to me as I collaborate with others.

Some people will disagree with me on the specific values I should use. In some situations, I will choose some values over others or rerank them accordingly. But more nefariously, some people will suggest that bad values are good and good values are bad. What should I do then? The key is to make sure that I understand the moral dangers and the potential for manipulation (as opposed to leadership), which is an inevitable concern when we talk of influencing others. What others do is up to them, and we can choose to follow them or not.

The question is, will (and perhaps should) people follow me? Vectors teach us that direction is central to leadership. Where leaders take people is important. How they take them there is important too. Our behaviors must be congruent with our values, and the tools we use (like the sources of power we pull from and the power tactics we use) must be in line with the values as well. It is an inescapable fact that leadership is a moral endeavor. Its values foundation is moral in nature. The directions leadership takes us have moral issues associated with them. The behaviors we engage in and the tools we use to influence others have both moral underpinnings and moral impacts on others.

As we engage with the practice of leadership, we are in the business of changing people's lives. The hope is that we change them for the better (and that we know what "better" really is).

Measuring Success

We now have a basis of determining the measures of success for both management activities and leadership. Like all good performance measures, the goal or purpose of the endeavor being measured is captured in the measurements we devise. To be as succinct and descriptive as we can, the measure of success of management is getting things done well. The measure of success of leadership is changing people's lives so that they can change or better accomplish the things that further our shared purposes (see Table 8.1).

Management's measure of success is all about accomplishing the tasks at hand and fulfilling the mission of the group. The focus is on things, as it should be in management. And the focus is on tasks as the focus should be given the purpose and underpinnings of management technology. Any focus on people is limited to only what they offer in terms of the tasks—their knowledge, skills, and abilities that management uses to get things done.

Whether it is done well or not is at the discretion of the management. Management determines standards, metrics, and processes. Management

TABLE 8.1 Measures of Organizational Success

Management	Getting things done well (we manage *things*)
Leadership	Changing lives for the better and getting things done because of the change in people (we lead *people* who then change things)

configures procedures and protocols that, if met, are sufficient for the activity and, if not met, are grounds for further managerial refinement. Such refinements can take the shape of retraining workers, reengineering processes, or redefining metrics. If needed, getting to the "well," as management defines it, may require wholesale change, reductions in force, reprioritizing business lines, and/or strategic reinvestments. But whatever the "well" is, it is management that both defines it and measures it. It is the great prerogative of management. And for some, it is the great allure of management positions as well.

The leadership measure of success is quite different, and not surprisingly, a little less quantifiable or fine-tuned. Changing people for the better, meddling in people's lives, and messing with people's values are the results and the intention of leadership. Measuring these results does not lend itself to reductionist, quantitative methods, but we seem to know when such change and influence have occurred, and certainly people have told story after story about their interactions with leaders in their lives that verify the measurement. We know when it has happened, though the extent is often unclear to everyone involved.

If there is some truth to the idea that the influence of leadership can occur and recur during people's lives, then it's even harder to measure. In other words, measuring leadership may not be a onetime event; leadership's influences can last a lifetime. What I encountered of leadership at a young age may impact me even more profoundly at a more mature age. In fact, the influence of leadership may live on beyond a person's lifetime. Perhaps that is why George Washington and Abraham Lincoln still inspire me. The end result of leadership is that lives have been changed.

A Moral Reminder

Here we must remember again the moral nature of trying to change people. History shows that changing people through leadership can sometimes have morally questionable results. We can argue whether a morally questionable result can occur from leadership activities (was it really leadership at all?), but the argument, if any, is based on the morality of the change effort and the sources of power used. It is based on the purpose and direction of the change. Was it ennobling or degrading? Was it enlightening or confusing and manipulative? For these reasons, the measure of the success of leadership must be in changing people's lives for the better. "For the better" matters and is a question of moral rights and moral wrongs, good examples and bad examples.

Let me share a personal story of what it might mean for leadership to change people's lives for the better. There are many examples from my own life for sure, and most come from my parents and family members. But to make the point more clearly, I will take an example from a different sample population: teachers.

This story is about my sixth-grade history teacher. He loved world history, and he loved teaching students how to learn it, and how to learn things generally. He would teach note-taking skills, listening skills, memorization skills, and test-taking skills, all the while making it fun for sixth graders. At one point in the year, I contracted an illness that caused me to be out of school for a month or so. My parents made arrangements for schoolwork to be sent home and for a few tutors to keep me up to speed on the work. In the middle of all of this, my teacher, of his own volition, made arrangements with my parents to help out in history. The deal he committed to? Every weeknight at 7:00 p.m. he would call me on the phone and give me that day's lecture, one on one, over the phone. What commitment! What caring! What influence he had! That example (and I will admit others) changed my life. It is a pretty big deal to devote that kind of effort for just one student. I did not fully understand the impact at the time, but his values, vision, goals, and respect for me as a person changed my life. He refined for me, through his example, certain values and ways of fulfilling them that were profound to me.

Let's be clear: he didn't add any new values in my life. Often leaders don't. You see, my mom and dad taught me to go the extra mile. My teacher showed me what that meant in ways my parents probably couldn't. He reinforced and at the same time refined those values I already had been exposed to and was learning to adopt. My dad would teach things like, "Work a dollar and 10 cents for every dollar you earn." Such phrases helped instill in me a work ethic. My teacher showed me what that meant in ways perhaps other people couldn't have. My mom and dad always taught me through word and deed to care about others, to help them, to serve in meaningful ways, and to understand that the individual matters. This teacher showed me what that meant through his actions and his unique example.

He messed with my values, by refining them. He meddled in my life, by showing me examples of commitment and concern. And in so doing he changed me for what I think is the better. Don't get me wrong. My parents did too, but so did this teacher's particular influence affect the direction and purpose of my life. My capacity to work on tasks and to affect change in the world (and in other people) changed because of it. That is what leaders do. They help others in such a way that as these followers choose to exert leadership on their own, they are able to help others get things done better, because they have been changed for the better.

Knowing whether we succeed in our leadership is often a tricky thing, and our success may be noticed only in stages and perhaps only on someone else's timetable. Take, for example, a Little League baseball team. How can a coach measure his success? If leadership were managerial in nature, he would measure success by how the players accomplished the tasks like hitting, catching, throwing, and scoring. This measurement is the first step in identifying the better players and the starters. Another measure may be the efficiency of schedules and practices, mapping out times, drills, and practice outlines. Ultimately, all of those measures pale in comparison to the one measure of success that matters most: winning games. Good coaches doing good leadership win games. At least that would be true if we attach management measurements to Little League baseball. Did we get things done well? Did we win games?

Perhaps, though, leadership has a different measure of success. Winning games is important, but perhaps the measure of success in the leadership (as opposed to management) of this team is simply a matter of changing the focus of your attention. Instead of aggregate comparisons, separating elements of the group into performance tiers, group schedules, and ultimately victories in games, we could focus on the individual and individual change over time. For the coach who has leadership success in mind, the measures of success may be less group oriented and more individually based.

Individually based success comes from helping that one player learn to hold the bat and helping other players support that player in that effort. Maybe helping a player stay in the batter's box when that ball is coming toward the player is another measure of success. Or maybe success is helping a player swing the bat once instead of striking out every time while looking as the ball passes by. Even helping a player swing and connect with a foul ball until eventually the player hits a ball in play can be viewed as success.

Being there while the player makes his first base hit, or her first catch in the outfield, and then celebrating success with them and their teammates are elements of leadership. All of this occurs without a run being scored yet, without any managerial evidence of success on the scoreboard. Nevertheless, there is plenty of evidence of personal growth, of increased capacity, and of individual strength. There is still plenty of evidence of leadership that changes lives.

An All-American athlete, who participated in track and field, told me once that at the beginning of the year, her coach held team meetings as an opportunity for each team member to get to know each other and begin to create a community dedicated to both academic and athletic excellence. She said that although academic and athletic goals spelled out in terms of statistics and awards were important to the coach, the coach always said, "My most important goal is not to coach great athletes, but to help you become great people." He recognized that success as a team is in large part dependent on a perspective that recognizes that team members were not just runners, but that they were unique individuals with a variety of skills and abilities that enriched the work of the team.

Accepting this view of leadership success, or even accepting such activities as leadership activities, may require some learning and changing over time. I recall the efforts of a nontraditional student trying to describe an example of leadership in his life. He initially thought that such an assignment would be easy. He was a longtime volunteer in civic groups with project after project under his belt. He was a noncommissioned officer in the Marine Corps. In fact, upon his discharge, he was the second-most decorated Marine in his regiment. But he struggled to come up with an incident of leadership, because, he confessed, most of what came to mind he eventually realized were examples of management.

Then he told the story of something that had happened just a few weeks before the assignment was due. He and his wife were considering how best to help his son succeed in school. Though smart and capable, their son was struggling with what they finally determined were poor study habits. Having identified the problem, he took the lead in fixing it—he would teach his son good study habits. Paraphrasing from his account, this is in essence what he said about a significant realization that he had regarding the measures of success of leadership endeavors:

> I approached this problem as I had many in my life, through management, and when that did not work, micromanagement. However, after sitting with [my son] and casually talking about my homework, why I do it, and why he should do it, the management I had intended to use to correct the problem turned into leadership based on principles. [My son] was very interested in why I was still going to school. I have a job, a house, and enough money (in his opinion) to do whatever I wanted, so why did I choose to go back to school? This gave me the opportunity to really explain to him the benefits

of education, of self-improvement, of developing a picture of where you want to be in your life and planning how to get there. While I had certainly preached all these ideas to him in the past, we had never really discussed them.

Instead of just ensuring that the work was getting done, I was able to instill in him a principle he had not had before. I was able to communicate a vision of the future to him. This vision allows him to adjust his methods to his future goals. With this new insight, he was able to gain a sense of personal resolve, a sense of commitment to a plan for achieving his ambitions.

Our conversations led him to a sense of identity, personal strength, emotional self-assurance, and self-esteem he had not had before. My inspiration had provided him guidance and direction where there had been none. More than showing him how to do the work, I had shown him why he should do the work. That's what real leadership is all about—not the how of getting things done, but the why.

Leadership *is* about the whys of work and of life. It is about individuals changing the lives of other individuals. It is about progress and growth, and in this case, as with many other cases, it is about love.

Where the Four Vs Take Us

We know when leadership is taking place and when it is successful. We can't always put our finger on it, but we know. The reason is that leadership is an individual issue; it is personal, and when we see leadership, we know it. The Four Vs of Leadership (see Figure 8.1) remind us that we learn more about leadership by looking at the followers than we do any specific person in a position of authority. The followers help us define who is and who isn't a leader.

Leadership is about how to get others to follow you (and not someone else), and therefore the measure of success is whether someone does. We know that leadership taps into the fundamental and individual capacity to choose that is innate in all of us. Leaders tap into the things that help us choose and provide a way for the choice to be made. Those choices have a lot to do with the values and principles we hold to be true and useful in our lives, the compelling nature of those values and principles in action in our lives, and the direction and magnitude of activity we must engage in to make those meanings and purposes a reality.

Values, vision, vectors, and voice offer us a complete framework of how to do leadership and what leadership looks like on others. We can analyze and diagnose leadership in terms of the kinds of values and sources of

FIGURE 8.1. The Four Vs of Leadership—Reprise

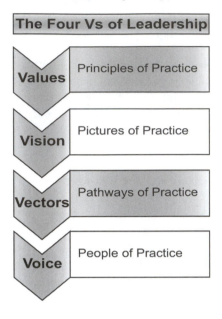

power being used in the relationships. We can choose some values and power sources over others, and we choose to follow some leaders and not others because of it. We can do the same in terms of the visions and stories used to explain those values in action. Certain behaviors and stories may not be congruent, may not be palatable to followers, and so choice enters in again. We can choose to like the values but not the vision and be a tepid follower, or we can buy into all of it and be that much more committed to the leader. Even more commitment can be garnered if the follower buys into the direction and type of work the leader outlines to fulfill our values and vision.

Again, this is a choice on the part of the follower, and it impacts what kind of follower, if a follower at all, he or she will be. Leadership is understood by seeing whether followers choose to agree, adopt, and act on the values, vision, and vectors presented. Once the choice to follow is made, the follower is still free to self-govern, but the self-governing is altered because the person is altered. The person has refined values, a crisper vision, a better sense of activity and direction to the work being done. The choices the follower makes become much more congruent with the choices the leader would make, because leader and follower are growing more united. The result is less control or power *over* others and more individual moral agency and power *with* others.

This view of leadership takes us away from some traditional approaches. It is not based on position or power, at least not fundamentally. It is not based on traits, behaviors, or situations—at least not essentially. This view takes us from an organizational view to an individual view that then explains the organizational dynamics more completely. It takes us away from a reductionist analysis of leadership (or management) components to a more holistic understanding of the leadership phenomenon as leadership and not as something else.

Defining leadership is indeed a bit tricky. As a leadership researcher once said, there are as many definitions of leadership as there are people defining the term. But leaving the definition of leadership up to the whims of people has gotten us into a definitional mess in the first place, a mess where so many have tried so long to say something of significance (without always succeeding) about this pervasive social phenomenon called leadership.

Remembering the story of a hermit, a young man, and a bird told in an earlier chapter, I suppose one way of looking at leadership suggests it is as you wish it to be. In that story, recall that the hermit suggested to the young man that the bird's condition was in the hands of the young man—it was as he wished it to be. You do get to choose whom you will follow. You get to choose to lead or not. It is up to you what your values are, and you get to define a vision for others to examine. Your vectors are put into play, and you impact the approach to voice you will adopt in association with others. Leadership is as you wish it in yourself and in others.

Yet leadership isn't simply as you wish it to be. There is something different about leadership and management and other social phenomena, for example, authoritarianism or oppression, or raw wielding of power. Leadership isn't amoral. There is a moral component of leadership, and so willy-nilly wishes are not sufficient grounding to analyze or engage in leadership. There is moral direction and hence moral hazard in leadership, and so doing leadership is not merely left up to what you wish. What you wish must be informed by moral rights and moral wrongs. If you wish to use hate and pride and power *over* as the values foundation to your leadership, then by natural consequence of those principles, what you will end up with is not a leadership relationship encouraging betterment and personal choice, but rather a relationship of control. Some interactions, though collective in nature and purposeful, are not necessarily held together by leadership.

No, leadership isn't merely as you wish it to be. Some social interactions are leadership and some are not. Calling the interaction leadership is not enough. It must actually be leadership. And that may be part of the confusion. For so long, we have given the leadership label to just about anything. If there was a group and it did something, then there was leadership. We have done even worse in giving the label "leader" to so many who really don't measure up to the notion. The words *leader* and *leadership* are used so often to describe people and phenomena that are so disparate that in some sense leadership has become an unknown. It has become, through no fault of its own, *merely* as we wish it to be.

The Four Vs of Leadership offers a framework that helps us know what leadership is and what it isn't. We can test each element to make sure leadership is what is really going on. We can test whether the values are the kind of values that foster leadership, management, or something else. We can test whether the vision is consistent and compelling, even noble. We can test the vectors to see whether the direction is congruent and the approaches sufficient. We can examine the commitment and implementation of voice in the relationship to see whether agency is honored, dismissed, or worse yet, destroyed.

As we choose to engage in the leadership relationship, as either leader or follower, let us remember that leadership is not just what we wish it to be. However, it is something to wish for more of in the world today.

Points to Ponder

1. How does leadership change people's lives? Should there be a "direction" to the change?
2. How is determining the proper measure of leadership and then measuring the individual *and* the organization useful?
3. How do you measure success in leadership?
4. Do you think that leadership is about the "whys" of life? Why or why not?
5. How do the Four Vs provide you with both a leadership analysis tool and a practical guide to leadership?

Quotables

1. "A good objective of leadership is to help those who are doing poorly to do well and to help those who are doing well to do even better." —Jim Rohn, businessman

2. "The first responsibility of a leader is to define reality. The last is to say thank you. In between, the leader is a servant." —Max DePree, author and businessman

3. "A small body of determined spirits fired by an unquenchable faith in their mission can alter the course of history." —Mohandas Gandhi

Practical Activities

1. *Leadership Journal.* Keep a journal for at least a period of two months wherein you reflect on your exercise of leadership. Reflect on your ability to be explicit about your values and articulate an aligned vision. Critique your vectors as needed. More importantly, reflect on your approach to followers regarding voice and the volunteer nature of leadership. Honestly evaluate the moral and ethical components of your leadership. Focus on your sources of power and how you define and measure success. Determine your perspective of leadership and whether your values and power sources make sense within that perspective. Make notes of any areas for improvement you may identify. If appropriate, share parts of your journal with a trusted confidant to gain more insight about your leadership from external sources.

Index

About the Author

MATTHEW R. FAIRHOLM is an associate professor with a joint appointment in the Department of Political Science and the W. O. Farber Center for Civic Leadership at The University of South Dakota. His academic and professional interests focus on public administration, leadership theory and practice, and constitutional governance. Dr. Fairholm worked in the U.S. federal government, entering the federal service as a presidential management intern. After several years in federal service, he joined The George Washington University's Center for Excellence in Municipal Management and remains a senior fellow there. For over 15 years, Dr. Fairholm has trained and consulted in a wide variety of organizations, with an emphasis on leadership and management development, strategic thinking, and public service. He holds a doctorate in public administration with an emphasis in leadership theory and practice from The George Washington University. His published works include *Understanding Leadership Perspectives: Theoretical and Practical Applications* (2009) and numerous professional reports and articles in public administration and leadership journals.